BRAINS

vast inland seas

Age of Anxiety

ANTISEPTIC

TOM SAWYER

palms peeled   COW

make ya shiver

exuberant spirit

He was blond   GELATOS

urban jungle

CHILD

alarm clock

WOMEN   BOAT

rebirth

warrior   PIE   milkweed

I cried a little bit

slipknot's drawn

when stars appear

Into love

prophetic toenails

watermelon   tropical smell

TESTIMONIAL

NSIBILITIES   hour on hour

and tide   Uncle Levi

time

languages   BAGEL

with emptiness   SQUEALS

brain is mush

borrowed from the sky

D.N.A.

Frogsly

fill the tub

bamboozled

AUTUMN   My face was wet

thrill machine

ARM

Stand up!

cooked rice   stroll

cover howls

carnival

GHOSTS

honeyed

POSTURE

packing sheds

so beautiful that couple

Fire   Listen to the skies

HUGE BIRD

two buses

fried corn   Clorox

next ferry to Alaska

Flag Ocean

MULTIPLYING

ng

COFFEE

Clinking rings   the bugga

shopping bags

halls of justice   stormy weather   WIND

billion

mirage   beer gut

MILKMAN

Lunch recess

lipstick on the collar

this galaxy of ours

difficult of men   DOG

HI MOM   part III

tomorrow's myths

there's no work

AHHHH   behold the charm

citrus yellow

the nerd let him have it

A word for nothing   CASH

BUS STATION

nization

and the quarters   Mama said

called Pagan

Arabies of hot meaning   I'm goin the store

EACH LEAF

everything comes down to this

tell our daughters   ordinary man

sparkling rush

er's love or loneness

CHOCOLATE

art   celibate

I open the library book

massive croon   Ahem

in the movies

this is the secret

Gulf of Spice

We could all get tattoos

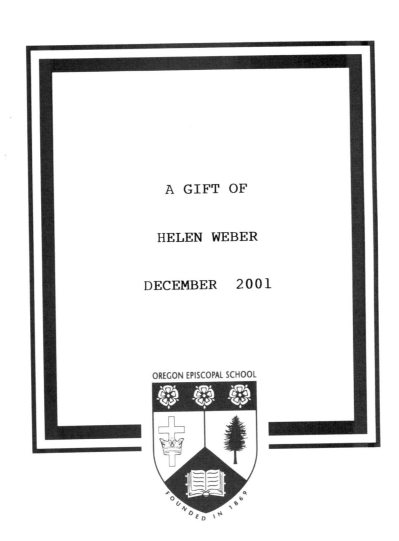

IF IT AIN'T A PLEASURE, IT AIN'T A POEM

—WILLIAM CARLOS WILLIAMS

LISTEN TO THE SKIES, LISTEN TO THE SOUNDS

SOMETHING ON THE LAND, SOMETHING GOING DOWN

–JOHN TRUDELL

Joshua Blum + Bob Holman + Mark Pellington

The United States of Poetry

HARRY N. ABRAMS, INC., PUBLISHERS

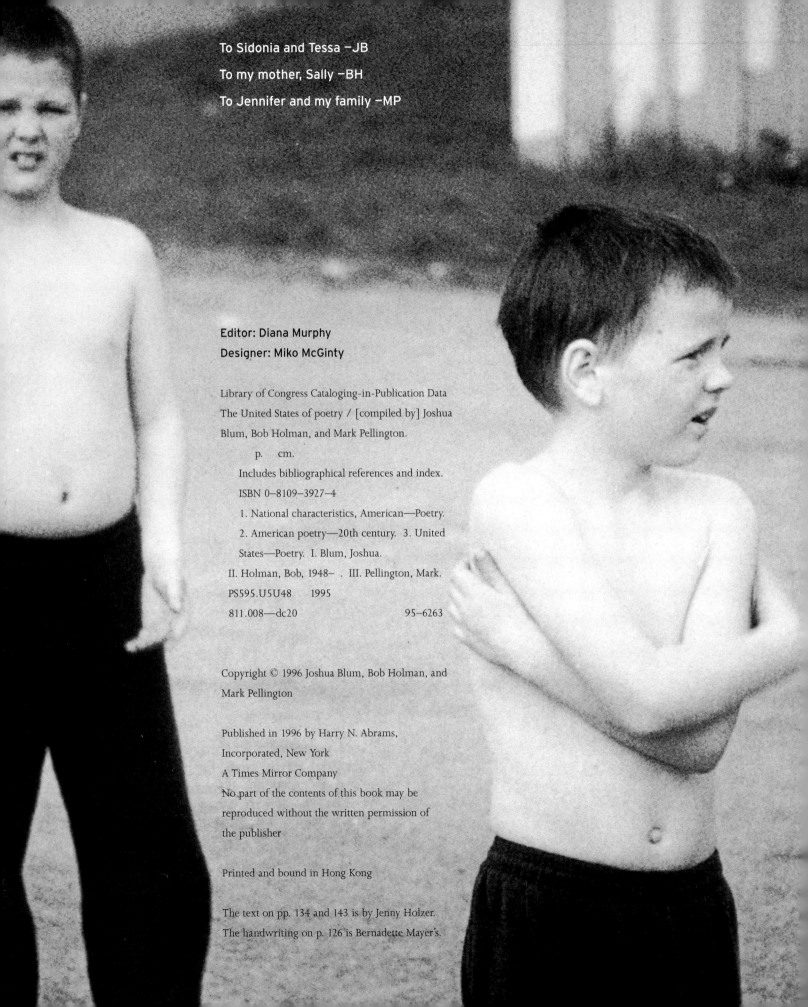

To Sidonia and Tessa —JB
To my mother, Sally —BH
To Jennifer and my family —MP

Editor: Diana Murphy
Designer: Miko McGinty

Library of Congress Cataloging-in-Publication Data
The United States of poetry / [compiled by] Joshua
Blum, Bob Holman, and Mark Pellington.
    p.   cm.
  Includes bibliographical references and index.
  ISBN 0–8109–3927–4
    1. National characteristics, American—Poetry.
    2. American poetry—20th century. 3. United
    States—Poetry. I. Blum, Joshua.
  II. Holman, Bob, 1948– . III. Pellington, Mark.
  PS595.U5U48   1995
  811.008—dc20   95–6263

Published in 1996 by Harry N. Abrams,
Incorporated, New York
A Times Mirror Company

Printed and bound in Hong Kong

The text on pp. 134 and 143 is by Jenny Holzer.
The handwriting on p. 126 is Bernadette Mayer's.

Welcome to The United States of Poetry!

In the waning days of the Second Millennium, in a time of madness and plague, it is extraordinary and heartening to begin to hear, through the noise of rhetoric-by-committee and the purpose-of-language-is-to-sell-something, the reemergence of the singular voice of the poem. Poetry, until recently considered an art all but extinct, is being reborn. No longer necessarily thought of as the dense and impenetrable domain of an elite, poetry is reentering our culture as something as familiar as a schoolyard rhyme, as exciting as the discovery that love can mean the same thing to two people.

This is a **book** of **two** firsts.

This is the first book of poems ever to be based on a television series.

And this is the first book containing every style and tradition of American poetry allowable within the abhorrent and anti-poetic limitations of space and time. Poems so varied they make you think of the plural, "poetries," or of music: jazz poems and classical, rap poems, country and western poems, rock and blues and experimental and...

Here, finally, is a collection of the "varied carols" that Whitman heard America singing.

These two firsts are related. Now that you can reach millions of TV viewers with a single poem,

Which **poems** would **you** choose?

These poems were selected to illuminate a country. Ours is a crucial mission, a healing mission. The U.S. has become a nation divided, splintered into a hundred nations. Without exception, the poetry of these cultures has been passed on within the individual cultures, defiantly, from voice to ear, often without being written down, and generally without being thought of as poetry. These traditions have been locked out of literature, while poetry itself has been relegated to a corner, painted in by definitions that have reduced an art to a footnote.

So here, of course, you will find the three U.S. Nobel Prize–winners for poetry (none of whom were born in the States) and our Poets Laureate. But you will also find rappers, slam poets, cowboy poets, street poets, poets who write in Spanish and Pidgin and Tlingit and Tagalog. Former President Jimmy Carter, whose first book of poems was published in 1995, is a citizen of The United States of Poetry, as is Robert Chambers, President of the Los Angeles Homeless Writers' Collective, and seven-year-old Sawyer Shefts of Salmon, Idaho.

The poets in The United States of Poetry are not "experts" explaining their traditions. Archibald MacLeish's famous lines,

> A poem should not mean
> But be

come roaring in at this point: some of the poems in this series may be emblematic of the poets themselves, of their varied voices; many are not. The integrity of the poem is what is essential, is what gives the poem force, as the poem is translated through another art. And it is respect for the individual, the individual voice and vision, that is the basis of poetry's power.

> Through these poems we can hear each other,
> begin to know each other, become acquainted with each other.

As we regain respect for the poets of our own cultures, we can begin to hear, understand, and respect the cultures and traditions of others.

> It is within television's power to reach into the nation's living rooms
> and reclaim our country's soul with poetry.

The Millennial Moment draws nigh! Are Yeats's spinning gyres (whose points, when they touch on 1/1/00, are to launch a New Age) actually Poetry and Television, those opposite arts?

Poetry is a single voice, TV is a hundred people performing arcane technical tasks behind a camera....A poem is words scribbled with a pencil nub on a bar napkin, a TV show is a million-dollar advertising opportunity....Poetry books are mimeo'd, hand-sewn, published by university presses; TV series are debated in popular magazines and spin off huge subsidiary industries....

The Beats and Plato

On November 30, 1959, the Beats were mentioned on the cover of *Life* magazine (although the cover image was from a story on "The Beauty of Postage Stamps"). The Beats created the notion that there was a lively alternative to the canon, an outsider tradition of anti-traditionalists centered in poetry, but since the early 60s, poetry has not been been heard from on the national stage.

It was Plato, in fact, who banned poets from his Republic. Because the poets' Truth refused to be acculturated, they were to be tolerated as powerless outsiders, whose words were important, but only as a kind of chorus outside the walls. In this country, for generations, poetry has been a creak on exhibit at the Dust Museum, something written by the Dead.

Why are **poets** being heard from **now?**

Poets today are beginning to face the center of the problem, the hole in the middle of the country where its soul once was. These poets are connecting with each other through the technologies that were to have spelled the end of literature. It's one thing to find Gwendolyn Brooks on the thirty-second band on an old Caedmon Spoken Word record; it's another to use a CD, or CD-ROM, point, click, and read the text as the poet reads to us.

So television and other media are providing a way for poetry to be seen and heard. There are five hundred channels with nothing on, and here is a group of people called poets who have so much content they can't be stopped. Shall we dance?

Rap, Slams, Cowboy Gatherings, ASL Poetry, L=A=N=G=U=A=G=E

Of all the phenomena connecting poetry to the popular culture, the most powerful is rap. A richly rhymed and rhythmic verbal construct that grew from the Hip Hop world created in the Black community of the South Bronx in the late 70s, rap is a new poetic form, between *pantoum* and *sonnet.*

To say "Poetry" in a high school class has been to induce immediate gagging motions followed by a glazed, zombie-like stupor. To say "Rap" is to be barraged by half-hour recitations from each student. To say "Rap is poetry" is to draw skeptical looks from both hard-core rappers and poetry purists, yet it is at the center of a new definition of poetry. Whether a certain rap is good or bad poetry is another question, but to deny a place in our nation's literary traditions to a brawling, sprawling, language-based art is to deny ourselves our heritage and our possibilities. Let us celebrate the richness and vigor of the American grain as it grows and changes to meet the Future. Or let us gag like zombies watching a gray box of Nothingness.

Another strand of new poetry began at Chicago's Green Mill Tavern in 1987, when Marc Smith found a home for the Poetry Slam. Smith, an ex-construction worker, loved poetry and its possibilities, and finally screwed up the courage to cross the cultural divide and attend a poetry reading—and lo, he was bored therein, and so did Smith create "Slam"!

Yes, the Poetry Slam, whose very name sends terror into the civilized. The Poetry Slam, those mock Olympics with judges selected randomly from the audience, judges who dare to score the poem between zero ("a poem that should never have been written") and ten ("a poem causing simultaneous orgasm throughout the audience"). But please use the Dewey Decimal System of Slam Scorification—if there's a tie, we must resort to the Dreaded Sudden-Death Spontaneous Haiku Overtime Round! With tongue in cheek (usually), and competition itself competing with irony and hype, the Slams have brought Whitman's "muscular art" pow upon the ear of the populace. The Slam is now the most potent grass-roots arts movement in the country, existing in over thirty cities, with an annual National Slam that attracts hundreds of poets. Chicago retains its position as Slam Central and even has an annual poetry-video slam and festival, organized by Michael Warr of the Guild Complex, Jean Howard, Quarish Ali, and Kurt Heintz. More than anything else, at a time when "poetry readings" connoted a beard chained to a podium, a muffled voice, and an airless ear, Slams allowed a generation to attend a poetry reading without saying they were going to a poetry reading.

The Nuyorican Poets Café in New York's Loisaida (Lower East Side) is a magnet for poets from all genres as well as being a springboard for the diverse collection of poets who have appeared on MTV and other networks, and as the center for a spoken word movement that is transmitted through tapes and CD's, CD-ROM's, live tours, and the continued publication of small press chapbooks and magazines like Steve Cannon's *A Gathering of the Tribes.* Co-directors Miguel Algarín and Lois Griffith, Roland Legiardi-Laura, Willie Correa, Sonia Lopez, and I preside over live music and theater programs, film-script readings, and visual art exhibitions, as well as the twice weekly Slams.

The largest poetry event in the country is probably the annual Cowboy Poetry Gathering in Elko, Nevada—"The Middle of Nowhere in the Middle of Winter." Organized by Hal Cannon and Sue Wallis and others at the Western Folklife Center, the five-day fest draws ten thousand people. Here poetry readings start promptly at 9 AM, with six readings per hour, five poets per reading, plus an open mike till 5 o'clock. All day you'll see western couples hunched over their programs, figuring out which reading to go to next. A tape duplication system is whirring away—you can grab up a cassette of your favorite reading just moments after it's over. In the evening, line up for the Big Show in the two-thousand-seat auditorium, which is completely filled—once for the early show, again for the late night. And while cowboy poetry is dedicated to revealing (and preserving) a way of life, it is as filled with just as many opinions on how to do that as any other poetry aesthetic. Check out the range wars between the classically rhymed poets like Wallace McRae and the free versification of Rod McQueary and Paul Zarzyski in John Dofflemeyer's *Dry Crick Review.*

In Rochester, Jim Cohn, Kenny Lerner, Debbie Rennie, and others began the American Sign Language Literary Conferences, which are a perfect metaphor for the new poetry: being composed in a visual language, the *only* way these poems can be "published" is on film. Or videotape. Clayton Valli, Patrick Graybill, Sam Supalla, Terrylene, Ben Bahan, and others are creating a new literature from this "new" language.

In Boulder, Allen Ginsberg, Anne Waldman, and Andrew Schelling oversee the Jack Kerouac School of Disembodied Poetics at the Naropa Institute. Here Beats' "spontaneous bop prosody" is taught in the only degree-granting Buddhist institution in the country. In many ways precursors of much of the current new energy of poetry, Naropa is a model for carrying on traditions that have heretofore been homeless.

At The Electronic Café in Santa Monica, Merilene M. Murphy holds court around the country via her vid-phone Telepoetics, and there are poets slamming on the Internet thanks to Sherry Rabinowitz, Kit Galloway, Dan McVeigh and his Senator Pobot, and Chris Funkhauser of *We* magazine. This blend of hi-tech ideology and lo-fi culture springs from the varieties of PerfPo that Ed Sanders instigated in the 60s and 70s, and continues on his one-man poetry-TV show, "The Sanders Report."

At the Ear Inn in New York, at universities from Buffalo to Berkeley, you will find the highly energized asyntactical purveyors of the Language School. Drawing from Charles Olson, the Objectivists, and Deep Image poets, these writers offer a rigorous, text-based, politically aware, and demanding aesthetic. The poets most influenced by Semiotics and Deconstructivism (although the sampling techniques of some rappers, and poets as diverse as Paul Beatty and Ted Berrigan, might belie this), the Language writers have found a way to outflank the academy with an avant-garde poetic rich in theory and exciting in practice. "Difficult" is one characterization of this work, but as Mark Pellington's treatment of Carla Harryman's "Fish Story" conjures, it is full of rewards when attacked boldly. Many well known writers here, to mention a few: Charles Bernstein, Barrett Watten, Lyn Hejinian, and Ron Silliman.

And what of the Academy? Surely, in the five hundred universities and colleges across the country, there are degree-granting writing programs that appreciate the flame of a new poetry. Many of the poets in The United States of Poetry teach, and the harder one tries to find the Academy, the more it disappears into a shroud of dust. The point of this book is to open up the definition of what a poem is, to have a chance to hear poets who speak to you, personally, to tune across an FM dial of poetries the way you can find music on the radio. Listen in to the alternative literary centers found in many locales—from Joe Flaherty's Writers and Books in Rochester to the National Writers' Voice Series organized by Jason Shinder, with outposts at Y's across the country, from Ed Friedman at the St. Mark's Poetry Project to Ray González at the Guadeloupe Arts Center, from Judith Roche at Seattle's Bumbershoot Festival to the Taos Poetry Circus of Anne MacNaughton and Peter Rabbit. "Poemfone," begun in New York by Jordan Trachtenberg, can now be found in San Francisco thanks to Gary Glazner and in L.A. thanks to Jayleen Sun and Mud Baron. Andrew Carroll has created the American Poetry and Literacy Project from the idea of then–Poet Laureate Joseph Brodsky and managed to put poetry anthologies in hotel rooms—over twenty-five thousand of them! ("The Bible can stand the competition," notes Brodsky.)

The poets are in town. The town is the country. The country is The United States of Poetry.

A Brief **History** of The USOP

When Josh Blum walked into the Nuyorican Poets Café in spring 1990, collaring me at the Slam to say that "this ought to be on TV," he set in motion an extraordinary chain of events. But first, as we say,

Flashback

In fact, up to the mid-80s, I had refused to own a TV or to allow a camera to record my readings. *TV was The Enemy*, the Skull Dozer, the Passivity Inducer. But when poet and friend Roberto Bedoya suggested TV producer Danny O'Neil contact me as a resource for a poetry TV series, my view of TV made an abrupt switch. Instead of the opponent, TV was to become an ally, a means of transmission, a collaborator. I had been involved with Rose Lesniak and Laura Vural in some early proto-poetry videos, but here was the chance: *If you can't barge into the nation's living room and put a book of poems in everybody's hand, how about if they turn on their TV's and find a poem there?* (Footnote: Danny O'Neil died of AIDS in 1988; "Poetry Spots" had six seasons at WNYC-TV, where it won three local Emmys.)

From Josh's and my connection came a demo, "Smokin' Word." Co-directed by Joel Blumsack (aka Baron von Blumenzack aka Zero Boy) and Rick Reta, and hosted by Matthew Courtney, "Smokin' Word" was a fistful of poetic energy. MTV turned down the idea (although allowing, "We think you're right. Meaning is making a comeback. Content will be big in the 90s. But poetry will never be on MTV!"), but the people at Public Television's "Alive from Off-Center" were enthusiastic. "Words in Your Face" was born.

Bob Holman, Allen Ginsberg, and Josh Blum, meditating.

Mark Pellington (standing, above)

is a central figure in this drama. Mr. Pellington is a visionary who saw immediately that pushing poetry through a camera would push the camera itself to a new place. After years at MTV creating what to many is that network's finest show, the freestyle international image-driven "Buzz," the very essence of what would become "MTV style," he began to look for the next step. "Words in Your Face," the first collaboration of Pellington/Blum/Holman through Washington Square Films, was hailed as a breakthrough for poetry and television. "Words" became the basis of our next project.

The **United** States of **Poetry**

For two years, while new poetry was building across the country like a wave of words, Josh and I sat in the office of Josh's Washington Square Films conspiring to get the wave into a TV studio. We were joined by Colette Coyne, whose extraordinary dedication and energy made us seem to be a whole office. We sent out many a copy of "Words in Your Face," which itself is still being used as a teaching tool in facilities across the country, from prisons to hospitals, high schools to literary centers. We wrote many proposals for funding. Mark was

Front row: Salmon, Idaho, poetry workshop. Middle row: Anne Mullen and the USOP road crew. Back row: Bitterroot Range of the Rocky Mountains.

hard at work on "Father's Daze," an expressionistic portrait of his father's battle with Alzheimer's disease. He would call in regularly with bursts of inspiration and to check if poems were still being written.

We received early support from the New York State Council on the Arts and the Greenwall Foundation. Things were looking grim, though, when, two years later, fall of 1992, we decided to, one last time, apply to Independent Television Service (ITVS) of St. Paul, who had already rejected us once for a single one-hour special.

The proposal was for a series. And as Josh developed the structure, certain concepts became immediately clear: to divide the country by region or aesthetic would preclude the very basis of what we were most excited about—variety, energy, voices. The themes we settled on are the chapters of this book.

Let's cut through the months of honing and phoning. The gradual turn from the utterly impossible (321 proposals were sent to ITVS) to the remotely possible (cut to 111) to the "why are we spending so much time on this, which will repay nothing" (9) to our being green-lighted, one of three proposals actually to be made.

After three years the prospect of making this thing was too scary to consider. Mark suggested we bring in a very talented producer, Anne Mullen, whom he had often teamed up with before. She set to work getting the project in gear, collaborating closely with Mark to put together the creative team that would fulfill the vision of the series. Over the next five months, eighty treatments were written, crews were hired, and arrangements were made for a twelve-week, 13,400-mile trip on a Dolly Parton tour bus accompanied by a fifteen-passenger van and a yellow Ryder truck full of equipment. USOP hit the road!

There are eighty poets and three editors in this book. But the images you'll be seeing are the result of extraordinary work by a talented and dedicated team of professionals acknowledged on the credits page. Particularly, however, the work of Director of Photography Thomas Krueger and Production Designer Steve Kimmel must be pointed out. Working closely with Mark, they helped create a look that's as dynamic as the poems they illuminate.

See the credits! Read the poems! Find poetry on your TV!

And hear, at last, the Book itself. The subtext of bringing poetry to television *is the text*: the hidden agenda is the Hidden Book, to bring people back to the rewards of reading poems for themselves.

For all of you who have been moaning about the unsingability of "The Star Spangled Banner," we herewith offer not only a **new national anthem but a new nation, conceived in language, and dedicated to the proposition that poets define it better than politicos**, *if only we could find the ears to hear with, the eyes to read.*

Bob Holman
New York City, 1995

Show One

Where you from? Ours is the New Land, the roots of our family trees criss-cross beneath continents and seas. We're a hyphenated people, blends and shades. Monolingual on the surface, we speak varieties of English—or should that be American?—with tendrils from Africa, Asia, Europe. We speak our own versions of Spanish and Tagalog and Cantonese and French, praise the land in Tlingit and Cherokee, watch TV shows in Hmong and Japanese. We are from the world, a condensation of cultures in a large and generous nation. We come together in the way that a poem is created. Unaccustomed ideas intermarry, unrelated images create a new vision. All based in language, in thought made real, in the invisible connecting web of words, deep in the American grain.

The Land and the People

THE
POETS

A Crow Indian
who lives on the land
where Custer had his Last
Stand, **HENRY REAL BIRD**
considers the Little and Big Horn
Valleys his living room. A former rodeo
cowboy, now a renowned cowboy poet, he
twists language like a river, sails the river with his
voice....**GEORGE ELLA LYON** is a poet, fiction writer,
and children's book writer who hails from Harlan, Kentucky,
and currently lives in Lexington with her husband and children.
With acute attention to detail, she allows a whole world into the briefest
of poems, a world where talk eddies into pools of meaning, where relationships
go back generations, where stories are repeated the way silver is shined....**JEFF
TAGAMI** lived for years in San Francisco working in the business and financial worlds
and learning about writing at the Kearny Street Workshop. He and his wife, the poet Shirley
Ancheta, have recently moved back to their homeland, Pajaro, just outside Watsonville, where they
live, write poems, and raise their two children....Where the poem meets the rap is the natural habi-
tat of **TRACIE MORRIS**. "Project Princess" is based on her experiences growing up in East New
York. Well known for her improvisational performance techniques, she tours often with the band
werdz-n-muze (*sic*). She is a Grand Slam Champ at the Nuyorican Poets Café and in 1993 was
crowned National Haiku Slam Champ....**LOIS-ANN YAMANAKA** is a poet and fiction writer, a
storyteller and literary provocateur. Born in Ho'olehua and currently living in Kahalu'u, she writes
in the most pungent and original dialect of any modern poet, a blend of mainland American, island
Pidgin, and classic Hawaiian....**NAOMI SHIHAB NYE** was raised in St. Louis and Palestine, and
currently lives in San Antonio. She is a children's book author, translator, and editor, with a mel-
lifluous voice and subtle performance style. She is accompanied in her video poem by her
father....Poet in Tlingit and English, **NORA MARKS DAUENHAUER** is from Juneau. Sixty-nine
years old, she published her first book five years ago...."The Hiparama of the Classics," **LORD
BUCKLEY** (1906–1960) defies genre categorization and is therefore at home in the USOP....He is
the author of *Red Letter*, founder of the One Size Fits All Movement, one of the Unbearable
Beatniks of Life, leader of protests against *New Yorker* poetry, co-publisher, with his wife, Ellen
Carter, of "The Eleventh Street Ruse," and "renowned street poet." Talking about **SPARROW**,
bemused and bearded Rumi of the New Age poetry scene, although he refuses to accept member-
ship in anything....The reggae patois unleashed in Dub poetry is the language heard both in the
streets of major U.S. metropoli and the dirt byways of the Caribbean. **EVERTON SYLVESTER** is a
founding member of the Green Card poets from Brooklyn, and many of his poems reflect on where
exactly "home" is. He is currently an English teacher in the New York City school system....**RITA
DOVE** was Poet Laureate from 1993 to 1995, and she used those offices to help poetry find its way
into the daily life of the American people. She teaches at the University of Virginia and won the
Pulitzer Prize for her poetry narrative, *Thomas and Beulah*, loosely based on the lives of her grand-
parents....The Old Man of the Mountains, the Poet Laureate of Appalachia, **JAMES STILL** is, at
the age of eighty-eight, the oldest poet in The United States of Poetry. He still lives in his log house
in Wolfpen, Kentucky, on the banks of Troublesome Creek, where he's lived since 1939, when he
was a human bookmobile for the Hindman Settlement School, carrying a box of books that he
would rotate among six mountain schools....

How much longer
Do you want
To be in the wind
Elk River's edge
There I am standin'
Lookin' for a feelin'
In the roar of the water
Come down river lookin' around
Feelin' gotta roam.

Driftwood feelin'
Floatin' down love river
Heart's way can't do
I'm catchin' a ride
Driftwood feelin'
Floatin' down love river
Heart's way can't do
I'm catchin' a ride
Floatin' down love river.

Somewhere
Between the reflection and the stars
Is the feelin' of life in love
Where you could hear
The stars in the wind
Feelin', twinklin', and flutterin'

In cottonwood leaves
Just a feelin' in the wind
In yesterday from days gone by
Can I have tomorrow
From yesterday, that I borrow?

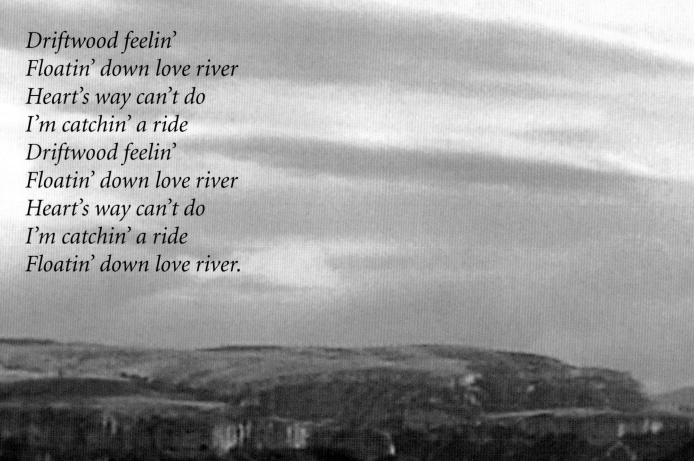

Driftwood feelin'
Floatin' down love river
Heart's way can't do
I'm catchin' a ride
Driftwood feelin'
Floatin' down love river
Heart's way can't do
I'm catchin' a ride
Floatin' down love river.

Driftwood Feelin'

Henry Real Bird

"...visit Paint Lick at my Uncle Levi and Aunt Bessie's...and that looks like Aunt Fanny, cousin Fanny and her children. This is the Mountain Laurel Fest and Grandmother Jo and some friends of the Robinsons'...great ideas of beauty and marching bands...and I don't know who this is, but it looks like Cindy LaPleux but Cindy's on the other side of the family so I don't know how she'd get in this album. You just never can tell..."

WHERE I'M FROM

I am from clothespins,
from Clorox and carbon-tetrachloride.
I am from the dirt under the back porch.
(Black, glistening
it tasted like beets.)
I am from the forsythia bush,
the Dutch elm
whose long gone limbs I remember
as if they were my own.

I'm from fudge and eyeglasses,
          from Imogene and Alafair.
I'm from the know-it-alls
          and the pass-it-ons,
from perk up and pipe down.
I'm from He restoreth my soul
          with a cottonball lamb
          and ten verses I can say myself.

I'm from Artemus and Billie's Branch,
fried corn and strong coffee.
From the finger my grandfather lost
          to the auger
the eye my father shut to keep his sight.
Under my bed was a dress box
spilling old pictures,
a sift of lost faces
to drift beneath my dreams.
I am from those moments—
snapped before I budded—
leaf-fall from the family tree.

George Ella Lyon

Pajaro the men

in fields that are not dreams

the tractor they must depend

Song of Pajaro

Pajaro the men thigh deep in mud
who are cutting cauliflower
the tractor they must depend
to pull them out
the catering truck selling hot coffee

Pajaro the children who clean
the mud from their fathers' boots
They sleep   They wake
to the smell of cauliflower growing
in fields that are not dreams
fields that begin under their bedroom windows
and end in a world they do not know
from the mountains to the river
from the river to the beach

Now Pajaro is tired   It wants to sleep
The packing sheds shut down for the night
The trucks close their trailer doors
and the Southern Pacific leaves town
(having got what it wanted)

This Pajaro of my mother leaving work
who at this moment is crossing the bridge of no lights
in her Buick Electra with wings like a huge bird
crossing over the black river toward home
where she will make the sign of the cross
over the cooked rice in the name of the Lord
and prepare for the table
a steaming plate of cauliflower.

Jeff Tagami

Pajaro the children

crossing over the black river toward home

where she will make

a steaming plate of cauliflower

Project Princess

Teeny feet rock
   layered double socks
      Popping side piping of
         many colored loose lace-ups

   Racing toe keeps up with fancy free gear
      slick slide and just pressed recently weaved hair

   Jeans oversized belie her hips, back, thighs
      that have made guys sigh
         for milleni-year

   Topped by an attractive jacket
      her suit's not for flacking, flunkies, junkies
         or punk homies on the stroll.

      Her hands mobile thrones of today's urban goddess
         Clinking rings link dragon fingers
            no need to be modest.

      One or two gap teeth coolin'
         sport gold initials
            Doubt you get to her name
               just check from the side
                  please chill.

         Multidimensional shrimp earrings
            frame her cinnamon face
               Crimson with a compliment if a
                  comment hits the right place

            Don't step to the plate
               with datelines from '88
                  Spare your simple, fragile feelings
                     with the same sense that you came

            Color woman variation reworks the french twist
               with crinkle-cut platinum frosted bangs
                  from a spray can's mist

            Never dissed, she insists:
               "No you can't touch this."
                  And, if pissed, bedecked fists
                     stop boys who must persist.

               She's the one. Give her some. Under fire.
                  Smoking gun. Of which songs are sung,
                     raps are spun, bells are rung, rocked, pistols
                        cocked, unwanted advances blocked,
                           well-stacked she's jock. It's all
                              about you girl. You go on.
                                 Don't you dare stop.

It's all about you girl. You go on. Don't you dare stop.

Tracie Morris

BOSS OF THE FOOD

Lois-Ann Yamanaka

Before time, everytime my sista like be the boss
of the food. We stay shopping in Mizuno Superette
and my madda pull the Oreos off the shelf

and my sista already saying, *Mommy,
can be the boss of the Oreos?*

The worse was when she was the boss
of the sunflower seeds.
She give me and my other sistas
one seed at a time.
We no could eat the meat.
Us had to put um in one pile on one Kleenex.

Then, when we wen' take all the meat
out of the shells and our lips stay all cho-cho,
she give us the seeds one at a time
cause my sista, she the boss
of the sunflower seeds.

One time she was the boss
of the Raisinettes.
Us was riding in the back
of my granpa's Bronco down Kaunakakai Wharf.
There she was, passing us one Raisinette at a time.
My mouth was all watery
'cause I like eat um all one time, eh?
So I wen' tell her, *Gimme that bag.*

And I wen' grab um.
She said, *I'ng tell Mommy.*
And I said, *Go you fuckin bird killa;
tell Mommy.*

She wen' let go the bag.
And I wen' start eating the Raisinettes all one time.
But when I wen' look at her,
I felt kinda bad cause I wen' call her bird killa.
She was boss of the parakeet too, eh,
and she suppose to cover the cage every night.
But one time, she wen' forget.
When us wen' wake up, the bugga was on its back,
legs in the air all stiff.
The bugga was cold.
And I guess the thing that made me feel bad
was I neva think calling her bird killa
would make her feel so bad
that she let go the bag Raisinettes.

But I neva give her back the bag.
I figga what the fuck.
I ain't going suffer eating one Raisinette at a time.
Then beg her for one mo
and I mean *one mo*
fuckin' candy.

Blood

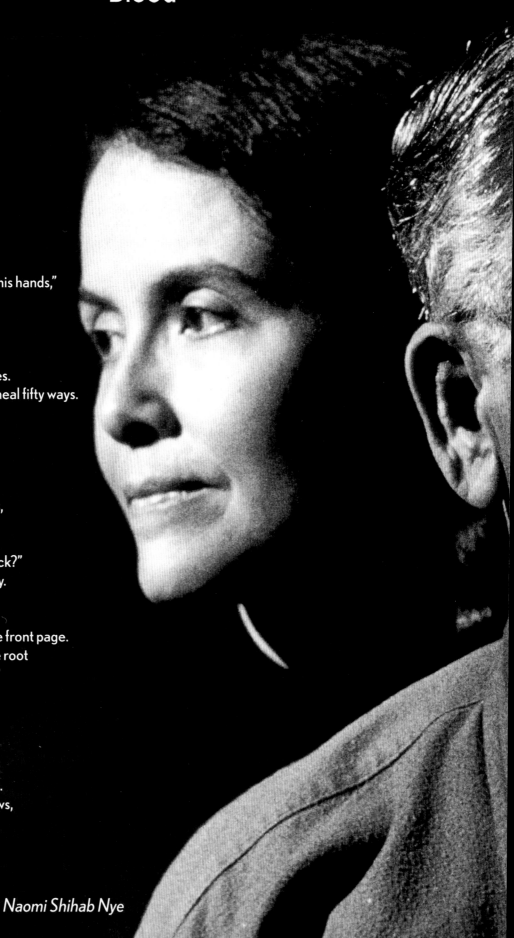

"A true Arab knows how to catch a fly in his hands,"
my father would say. And he'd prove it,
cupping the buzzer instantly
while the host with the swatter stared.

In the spring our palms peeled like snakes.
True Arabs believed watermelon could heal fifty ways.
I changed these to fit the occasion.

Years before, a girl knocked,
wanted to see the Arab.
I said we didn't have one.
After that, my father told me who he was,
"Shihab"—"shooting star"—
a good name, borrowed from the sky.
Once I said, "When we die, we give it back?"
He said that's what a true Arab would say.

Today the headlines clot in my blood.
A little Palestinian dangles a truck on the front page.
Homeless fig, this tragedy with a terrible root
is too big for us. What flag can we wave?
I wave the flag of stone and seed,
table mat stitched in blue.

I call my father, we talk around the news.
It is too much for him,
neither of his two languages can reach it.
I drive into the country to find sheep, cows,
to plead with the air:
Who calls anyone *civilized*?
Where can the crying heart graze?
What does a true Arab do now?

Naomi Shihab Nye

305 Belliman Road

Our farm is 25 miles outside of town

34 South Stone

keep going past the stop sign and my house is on the curve on the left

175th Street

7776 Mt. Tamalpais

the corner of Locust and Marietta

964 Ten Mile Road

421 Lafayette

2000 Pennsylvania Avenue

I live in the city

10 W. 19th St.

I live near the ocean

33 Hillman Avenue

A POEM FOR JIM NAGATAAK'W (JAKWTEEN)
MY GRANDFATHER, BLIND AND NEARLY DEAF

I was telling my grandfather
about what was happening
on the boat. My father
and his brothers were trying to
anchor against the wind
and tide.

I could smell him, especially
his hair. It was a warm smell.
I yelled as loud as I could,
telling him what I saw.
My face was wet from driving
rain.

I could see his long eyebrows,
I could look at him and get
really close. We both liked this.
Getting close was his way of
seeing.

Nora Marks Dauenhauer

Train's now leaving for Rosedale, Goldsdale, Flipsdale, Jam City, Rass Cross, Criss Cross, Ratitude, Latitude, Baditude, Hatitude, Nogsley, Dogsley, Frogsly, Hamstown, Bamstown, Your Town, My Town, Way Place, Say Place, Gay Place, Roptne, Vautne, Friptne, Shniksnaw, Krascraw, Assavaw, Avalanche, Pownspay, Pasville, Dasville, Hosville, Parsville, Krende, Bende, Senha and Krutne...

Now leaving on Track Twelve...

BOARD!

Lord Buckley – "The Train"

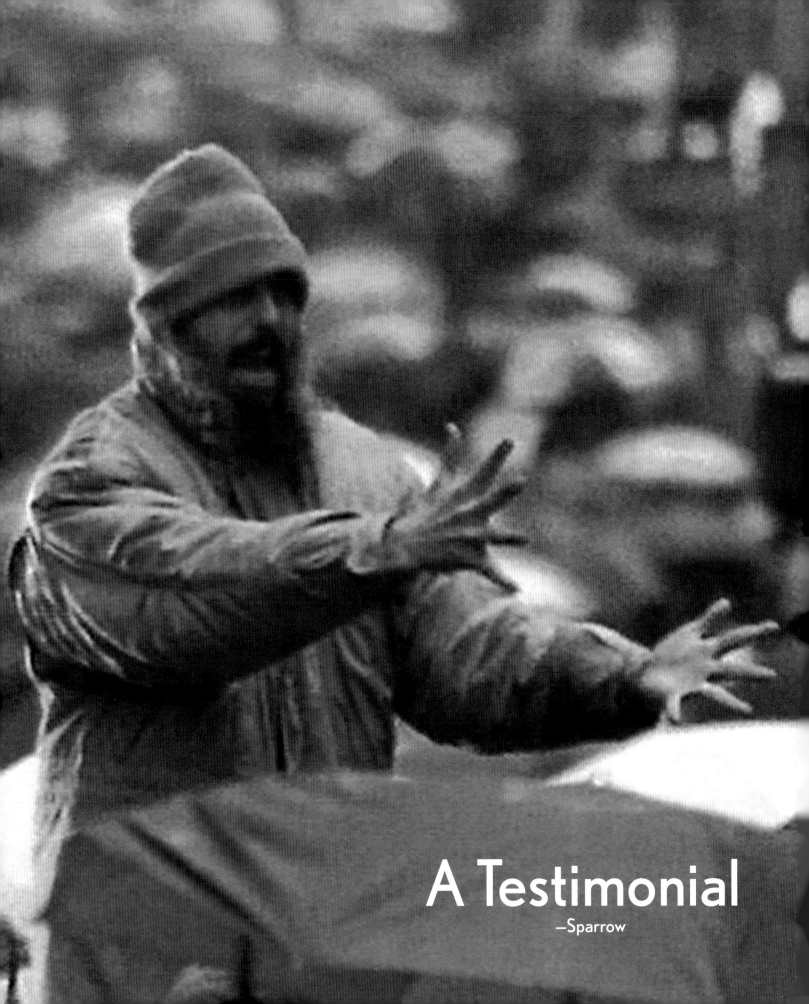

A Testimonial
—Sparrow

I have lived in this city

for 25 years
and all that time
I have dropped things.
I've dropped
tissues,
letters from women
in Santa Fe, N.M.,
money,
the keys to my house,
books by
Jacques Prevert.

And all this time,
you,
the people of this
city, have pointed
to me, and said,
"Hey!" "Sir!" "You!
You dropped something!"
and then I've picked it up.
You have watched
over me all these
years,
and I've waited till
now to thank you.

I rise each day
to yet another shock
from dis alarm-clock culture.
And I miss de sound
of mi big red cock
as him beat him chest
and crow welcome song
to de sun
from de fowl-shit covered
guava tree pon de hillside.

And de snooze button allow me five minute
more to dream bout ackee and breadfruit.
Den I get up and eat a bagel
and worry bout mi love handle.

Six layers a clothes
and termal drawers
and I still cold.
Another bridge mean more toll.
And de golden rule
is alternate-side parking.

dally

And as de belly get fat
many tings bout Yard dat
used to be just a mere inconvenience
start to look like major incompetence.
Unscheduled power cut
daily
water lock off
bank pon short staff cause
the morning was a little bit rainy.
Few telephones
dat's just how it is
yet everyone know
everyone else business.

Well I live in mi building for five years now
and mi neighbours dem still don't know me.
But solace come from anonymity.
And every time I bite de apple
de apple swallow me.

So dem force me to buy
a piece of the FBI-
CIA investment pie.
And dem give me a W2
form in lieu
of a receipt.
So now I'm funding a plot
to get God shot
or someting like dat.

De Korean polish him apples dem clean
and arrange dem in stacks of red, gold and green.
Say him want Rasta to feel welcome. Seen?

Still I yearn for de breeze
from de Natty Bay sea
as it cool down de sweat pon mi back
Long to feed dry coc'nut to mi cock.

So I dilly
and I dally
and I wonder
how much longer
I can philander
Cause each time I bite de apple
it swallow a piece of me
Still it hard to love de fruit
if I never did climb de tree.

Everton Sylvester

Silos

Like martial swans in spring paraded against the city sky's

Like martial swans in spring paraded against the city sky's
shabby blue, they were always too white and
suddenly there.

They were never fingers, never xylophones, although once
a stranger said they put him in mind of Pan's pipes
and all the lost songs of Greece. But to the townspeople
they were like cigarettes, the smell chewy and bitter
like a field shorn of milkweed, or beer brewing, or
a fingernail scorched over a flame.

No, no, exclaimed the children. They're a fresh packet of chalk,
dreading math work.

They were masculine toys. They were tall wishes. They
were the ribs of the modern world.

Rita Dove

I shall not leave these prisoning hills
Though they topple their barren heads to level earth
And the forests slide uprooted out of the sky.
Though the waters of Troublesome, of Trace Fork,
Of Sand Lick rise in a single body to glean the valleys,
To drown lush pennyroyal, to unravel rail fences;
Though the sun-ball breaks the ridges into dust
And burns its strength into the blistered rock
I cannot leave. I cannot go away.

Being of these hills, being one with the fox
Stealing into the shadows, one with the new-born foal,
The lumbering ox drawing green beech logs to mill,
One with the destined feet of man climbing and descending,
And one with death rising to bloom again, I cannot go.
Being of these hills I cannot pass beyond.

James Still

Being of these hills I cannot pass beyond

Show Two

To sleep perchance to dream—to wake up and it's off to work. The tick tick of the clock tock tock, the beat beat of the heart, the crash crash of the waves against the shore—the methodical irresistibility of time marches on. But when you look up from the computer screen and see the reflection off the water cooler, when you step out-side to have a smoke and the symphony of the streets suddenly strikes a major chord, when the teacher's barking stops and sheer silence envelops the classroom, when the smell of the manure signals growth and the warmth of the sun is skin itself—the poetry behind time's inexorability can strike at any moment. The poetry of the moment gives meaning to the hour, and the actual writing of a poem engages the richness and complexity of life. Here is a day in the life of The United States of Poetry, just one of the 24 segments that cycle every 7 days over a period of 365 every year. Each one just like the one before and the next, each one as different as night and day.

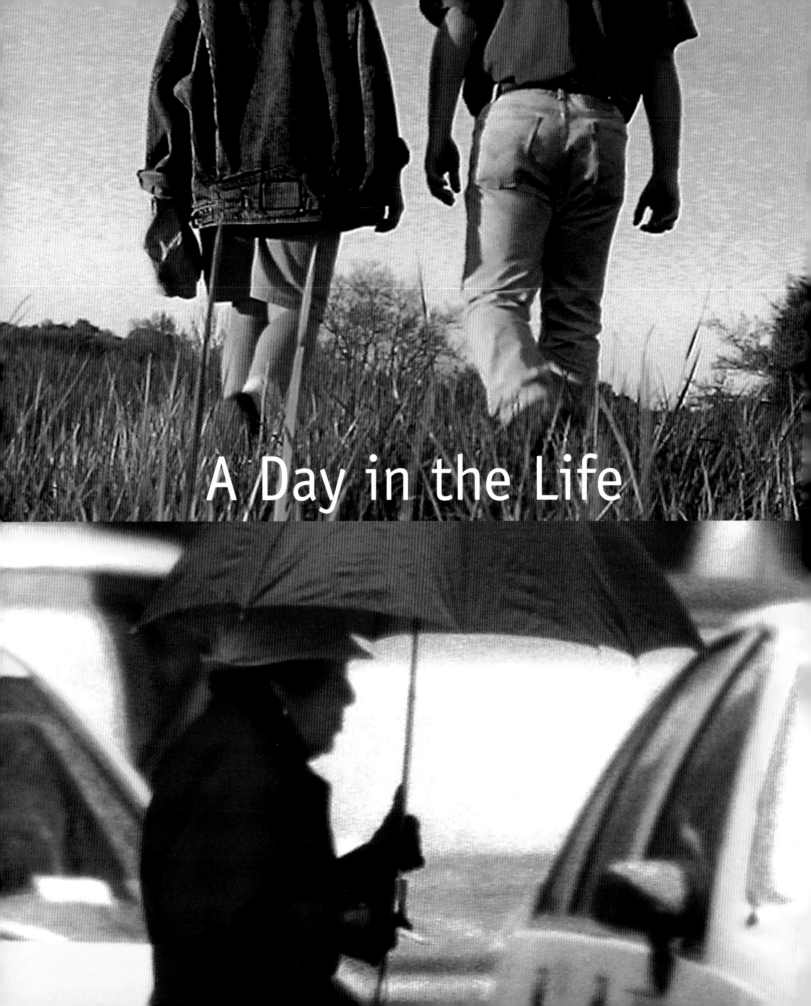

A Day in the Life

12

THE POETS

THYLIAS MOSS, author of six books,
lives, teaches, writes, and occasionally wins prizes
(her husband and sons impressive among them and quite unlike
the literary honors) in Ann Arbor, Michigan....CZESLAW MILOSZ, winner of
the Nobel Prize for Literature, was born in Lithuania and grew up in Poland. He
is known as a poet of truth—his visions of war are harrowing portraits of suffering, of
humanity somehow coming through inhumanity, and vice versa. He lives and teaches in
Berkeley....The guy on the elevator is PETER SPIRO, born and raised in Sheepshead Bay, Brooklyn,
whose poems are litanies of sense culled from a life on the streets. Whitman with a Brooklyn accent,
he has published five chapbooks of his poems....In a recent performance at Lincoln Center, Reverend PEDRO
PIETRI finally gave himself a promotion: he is now Bishop Pedro! A fixture on the streets of Nueva York, Pietri
sells poems with condoms as a living art performance—and a way to break even with life....A young rapper who
goes by the name Invisible Man (ISMAIL AZIM EL) was a finalist in the National Slam in San Francisco and won the San
Francisco Lollapalooza Slam, which enabled him to tour with the alternative rock fest. He appears to be in his early
twenties. We know no more except through his work—rap-based, forceful, and clear....You are looking over merchandise
at the Goodwill Store in Missoula, Montana, touching the lives of those who once inhabited these coats and shoes. Not
"Twilight Zone": this is a poem by Missoulan SHERYL NOETHE, whose work resonates deeply, a kind of soul-to-soul recy-
cling. Sheryl has taught poetry to deaf kids in New York, hearing kids in Salmon, Idaho, and head trauma survivors and other
developmentally disabled individuals in Missoula....The Cook Boys have been known to sit on tiny curbs outside 7-11's in
Milwaukee and trade bits of wise-cracking venom they call "poems." MATT COOK (who reads his poem in USOP) might be their
leader, although he isn't going anywhere thinking "James Joyce was stupid." They are unpublished....We were sent a mimeo
magazine from Nashville, and one of the poems, "Morels," struck a chord. We'd never heard of the author, DAN POWERS, but
located him at work at the TVA. He sent us a video of himself reading the piece, about his friend Vantrease who had to leave
his farm and go to work at the Sears catalogue store. The reading was extraordinary, and thus Dan, father of three, regular
at the Nashville Open Mic scene, finds himself a citizen of The United States of Poetry....One of the stars to rise from the
Nuyorican Poets Café is HAL SIROWITZ, a native of Flushing, Queens. He was awarded an NEA Fellowship in Poetry in
1994, the MacDowell Colony has had him in residence, and through it all he keeps on teaching his special-ed grade
school students back in Queens. Hal has recently appeared on MTV's "Spoken Word Unplugged"....PAUL BEATTY is a
native of L.A. currently residing on the Lower East Side and the author of two books. He is the T. S. Eliot of his
generation....Professor of Creative Writing at Brown by way of the Ozarks, C. D. WRIGHT edits, with her husband,
the poet Forrest Gander, Lost Roads Books. Poet Laureate of Rhode Island, she is curating an exhibition for
the state of Arkansas called *A Walk-In Book*, which incorporates letterpress broadsides of poems, pho-
tographs, videos, and crafts to evoke the arts and the artists of the state....The supercharged fiction
of DENNIS COOPER is well known as the way in to understanding the gay way of S & M, sex and
violence, drugs and decadence, American 90s L.A.-style. Dennis is a contributing editor at
Spin; his poetry is less well known, but extremely powerful, sometimes hard to
read—it makes you flinch with understanding....DEREK WALCOTT won the
1992 Nobel Prize in Literature. He lives in Brookline, Massachusetts,
and teaches at Harvard; his luminous writings evoke the cul-
tural diversity and richness of the Caribbean,
where he was born....

Get up in the morning 'bout a quarter to six
(get up up)
First Sergeant was pitchin' a fit
(get up up)
NCO's all around his desk
(get up up)
First Lieutenant and a Lady in Red
(get up up)
Feelin' tall and lookin' good
(get up up)
Oughta be in Hollywood
(get up up)

I left my girl back home in Alabama
 I left my girl back home in Alabama
And I know she's still there waiting for me
 And I know she's still there waiting for me
She's all right
 She's all right
She's OK
 She's OK
She's motivated
 Motivated
Dedicated
 Dedicated
Oh Yeah
 Oh Yeah

I get up when my cat gets up

the dawn,
Emblem of the day which hath no end.

—Richard Henry Dana
"The Husband and the Wife's Grave"

I wake up 'bout 7:30, have a cup of coffee, shower, shave, etc.

I get up about six o'clock in the morning...get to work

I hav'ta be at school at 7:45

*Let me clear up a nagging misunderstanding: This
is the way to make the white woman's bed; she thinks
I make it because she is rich, she thinks I make it
to get her money, that I can't get money any other
way, no skills, no intelligence, no contribution to
society but for her four poster, but I make her bed
because on Judgment Day, you will have to sleep
in the bed you made and I make damn good ones but
she didn't make any.*

NAGGING MISUNDERSTANDING

Thylias Mos

Gift

Dar

A day so happy.

Dzień taki szczęśliwy.

Fog lifted early, I walked in the garden.

Mgla opadla wcześnie, pracowałem w ogrodzie.

Hummingbirds were stopping over honeysuckle flowers.

Koliby przystawaly nad kwiatem kaprifolium.

There was no thing on earth I wanted to possess.

Nie bylo na ziemi rzeczy, którą chcialbym mieć

I knew no one worth my envying him.

Nie zualem nikogo, komu warto byloby zazdrościć.

Whatever evil I had suffered, I forgot.

Co przydarzylo się zlego, zapamnialem.

To think that once I was the same man did not embarrass me.

Nie wstydzilem się myśleć, że bylem kim jestem

In my body I felt no pain.

Nie czulem w ciele żadnego bólu.

When straightening up, I saw the blue sea and sails.

Prostujac się widzialem niebieskie morze i żagle.

Czeslaw Milosz

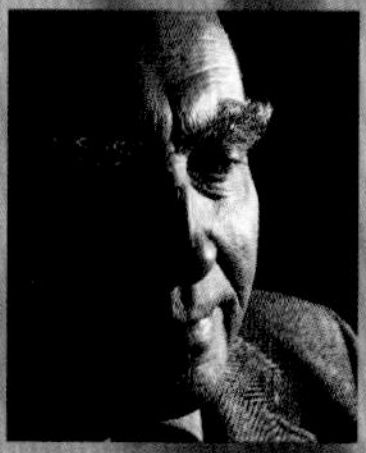

I

They say,
   What would you like to do
or where would you like to work
    they chop my solid twenty-four into segments.
You get two hours for waking, showering, eating.
One to two traveling then at least
eight there.
One to two more traveling home
supper a quick fuck or three beers
then sleep eight and
wake up again to shower, eat, travel, work, travel, quick fuck,
sleep, wake, shower until they merge and flow like
molten lava and I say,
    Yes, but I get two weeks vacation
    per year, ten holidays, twelve
    sick days and one floating personal
    day to live and I feel
like the negative space between the bars of a jail cell
that farts freedom in your face.
    These men, shelling out salaries
    of death sandwiches
    for my half-hour lunch break.

2

They say,
   What would you like to do
or where would you like to work.
   I think, Earth. I'd like to work
   on Earth, third in from the sun.
Does the bear say,
   I work in this section of forest.
Does the eagle say,
   I work in this part of space.
Does the shark say,
   I swim only here.
Does the air work or the wind.
   And what kind of work do I want to do?
I say,
   I want to eat and sleep and explore
    like the bear and the eagle and the shark.
I want to speak like the wind and breathe air
    period.
I want to hang a sign on my door:
   Do not disturb while I'm at work
    dreaming.
They say,
   this is lazy.
They say,
   you are worthless.
They say,
   you have no ambition.
And I tell them,
   I am an unambitious worthless problem
like the air and the wind.
I will sleep and dream like the air and
move in passion like the wind
when it pleases me and for
no one.

3

They say,
   What would you like to do
or where would you like to work.
They tell me,
   Do something you like to do,
   life is wonderful when you
   like your job.
I tell them,
   It is an oxymoron to like
   your job
   as if a convict ever loves
   his cell.
They say,
   Learn to drive a tractor trailer or fix
   automobile transmissions or
   learn to weld or fix toilets
   or serve drinks with paper umbrellas to people under the
shade and I think,
No one likes to work
the name itself implies
contempt, a comfortable
   contempt like the old convict who
   after years
   accepts his cell as home.
Some people like their jobs,
they say
   and I think,
     Who?
Who likes their job?
Does the garbageman really like picking up shit all day?
Do tellers like to sit all day behind a bulletproof
glass wall?
Even poets don't really like to teach workshops.
(I have heard them say this)
Fill ketchup bottles, stuff sausages, clean pots
or sell hot dogs and cigarettes.
And if you say,
    Doctors love their work or dentists love
their work or lawyers or engineers or stock brokers
then why,
   why do they value their
vacations as much as the
garbageman and the teller and the sausage stuffer and
the pot cleaner?
Baseball players like their work
some actors and poets and
all sleepers
who dream.

4 What kind of things perpetuate work?

Cancer,

yes cancer makes work.
It makes work for surgeons and people who run
self-examination breast programs.
It makes work for social workers and therapists
and nurses and chemical manufacturers and the people
who clean the floors in hospitals
and those who make the paper cups in hospital
bathrooms and makers of
high fiber cereal
and companies who advertise for
high fiber cereals and

morticians and casket makers and
people who supply the metal for
ash carrying urns and for the miners
of iron ore used for metal
ash carrying urns

and for florists and greeting card companies.
It makes work for
wig makers and sellers of wigs
and for plastic tube makers
and journalists and typesetters
and single parent rap group organizers
and ecologists and environmentalists
and lab technicians
and surgeons and people who run
self-examination breast programs.
Oh, I've said that already.

WORK

5 Factories would close without

workers

but plants would still grow
wind would still blow
mountains would still fold.

Without prison guards there would be
no prisons.
And doctors could not work without
orderlies and secretaries
the dry cleaners
the house cleaners
the supermarket stock boys
the tellers
the mechanics and the fixers of
automobile transmissions and toilets.

Armies could not function without
foot soldiers.

We have set this nightmare into motion and
we can stop it.

Quit!
Fighting for full employment is not the answer.
Fight for full
unemployment.
Everybody,
set your alarm for noon or turn it off and sleep
until you want to get up.
Bears do this, cats do this, birds do this,
so why should we be any different
inhabitants on this third planet in
from the sun
somewhere spinning and revolving in the
universe
yes, the universe is not up there
it's here
and we are in it.
Quit and sleep.
Sleep and dream.
Stop it
stop it
you're killing me.

Peter Spiro

Telephone Booth
905 1/2

Pedro Pietri

woke up this morning
feeling excellent,
picked up the telephone
dialed the number of
my equal opportunity employer
to inform him I will not
be in to work today.
"Are you feeling sick?"
the boss asked me
"No Sir," I replied:
"I am feeling too good
to report to work today.
If I feel sick tomorrow
I will come in early!"

My mother, your mother,
lives across the bay
She takes tea in East L.A.

12:12 pm

Oh mother dear,
see here, see here,
We have found our mittens

12:21 pm

Recess!

Lunch at 11:50

I go to the bank at lunchtime

I like to feed pigeons in the park

I don't even get up some days

51

I WAS READING FROM THE MOTHER OF BOOKS THE OTHER DAY
INSIDE THIS SACRED BOOK IT SAID
"THOSE WHO DO NOT SUBMIT TO THE WILL OF RIGHTEOUSNESS,
WILL DWELL IN THE FIRE, WHOSE FUEL IS MAN AND STONE"

AND AS I LOOKED OUTSIDE MY WINDOW,
I REALIZED–
THAT IT IS SO HOT TODAY.

IT IS SO HOT TODAY
THAT

A FIRE-BREATHING DRAGON DISGUISED AS A PROSTITUTE
IN A SEE-THROUGH MINISKIRT
WAS LAST SEEN IN AN ALLEYWAY, WITH THE DEVIL
SMOKING SYNTHETIC HEAVENS

AND ON THE CORNER OF FILLMORE and McALLISTER ST.
A 12-YEAR-OLD GIRL WAS MISTAKENLY SHOT
GETTING OFF THE 22 BUS
BY A .22 GUN
FROM A 22-YEAR-OLD BOY
FOR A DRUG DEAL UNDER 22 DOLLARS,
WHICH CAUSES A SORROW EXCEEDING THAT
OF 22,000 ANGELS SLAIN...

IT IS SO HOT TODAY.

IT IS SO HOT TODAY
that **ICE CUBE** and **BILLY D** are **SELLING**
LIQUID CEMETERIES electronically **TRANCE**mitted
SPONSORED BY the **C.I.A.** formerly known as the S.S.

AND NIGGAZ THINK EVERYTHING
COOOooool
WHILE NEW BRUNSWICK SNOWS
STING MY FEET LIKE NUCLEAR WINTER.

IT IS SO HOT TODAY
THAT THOSE WHO DO NOT SUBMIT
WILL DWELL IN THE FIRE
WHOSE FUEL, IS
MAN and **STONE.**

Ismail Azim El

Our boys are **F-I-N-E** "fine"
On the **L-I-N-E** "line"
and we **L-O-V-E** "love" them
all the **T-I-M-E** "time"

to the shortstop, home for one,

then off to Quintana for two

(crowd roars)   3:34 pm

Well, there's Hooker,
there's Honker,
there's Five to Stay Alive,
Beat 'em to the Bank

3:34 pm

GOODWILL THRIFT STORE, MISSOULA

It's hard to hate
anybody when we're
all maybe trying
on the shoes of the
dead together,
trying on their slacks
and reading their books.
So we are gentle
to each other
when we reach for the same glass
or same blanket.
Smile when we collide
between the broken couch
and a stain on the sheet.
We pass, cool ghosts who feel
the sleeves of jackets,
the hems of dresses, and hold
nylon stockings up to the light.
An old man tries on
a dead soldier's coat. It weighs
him down, he bends as though
he were carrying the man on his back.
When he opens his narrow pocketbook
a moth flies up.
We find blouses for our mothers
we never sent.
A past we never knew. White bowls
that fit inside each other.
Someone else's babies.
Painstakingly embroidered pillowcases.
Empty jars. Proof of happier lives.

When I walk past the rack
of dark wool suits
I smell a human musk
like an animal would.
I get a sense of a man,
of my long-dead grandfather,
and am filled with love
for the suits, love
for the man holding
the double boiler,
love for the teen-aged girl
with bare feet, sucking the ends
of her hair and watching
the clock, love
for the lonesome one
that the shoes
will surely
fit.

Sheryl Noethe

James Joyce

He was stupid

He didn't know as much as me

I'd rather throw dead batteries at cows than read him

Everything was going fine before he came along

He started the Civil War

He tried to get the French involved, but they wouldn't listen

They filled him up with desserts

He talked about all the great boxers that came from Ireland

Like he trained them or something

Then he started reading some of his stuff

Right as we told him to get lost

He brought up the potato famine

We said "Your potatoes are plenty good"

"Deal with it"

"Work it out somehow"

Then he said "America must adopt the metric system,

it's much more logical"

We said "No! We like our rulers, go away"

Thomas Jefferson said you always get the rulers you deserve

Matt Cook

There comes, it seems, and at any rate
        through perils, (so many) and of a vexed life,
The gentler hour of an ultimate day.

                            —Ezra Pound
                "Homage to Sextus Propertius"

Two years ago my friend, Vantrease,
said farming would not pay his bills;
he sold his milk cows,
leased the Sears Catalogue Store in town.

Blackberry vines and sumac
crowd the unkept pasture
and the fences sag.
Last week at church
he held out his hands
soft and white for us to see
and said, "A farm is like
the strength in a man's hands,
you try hard to keep it
and you lose it."

In the trillium beneath
the hickory grove on our ridge
my son and I find a few morels
and drop them into a brown paper bag.
Our small talk worn thin
we walk back to the house
through the dew wet pasture
without speaking.

Here, miles from town, without
his friends to see, he reaches
across our silent striding
in the bright spring morning
and grasps my hand with all
the strength of his ten years.

Each of us holds on.

Morels

Dan Powers

Crumbs

Don't eat any more food in your room,
Mother said. You'll get more bugs.
They depend on people like you.
Otherwise, they would starve.
But who do you want to make happy,
your mother or a bunch of ants?
What have they done for you?
Nothing. They have no feelings.
They'll eat your candy. Yet
you treat them better than you treat me.
You keep feeding them.
But you never offer me anything.

Hal Sirowitz

Seven o'clock when
the shooting stars start and
you hear it practically all night

7:03 pm

7:03 pm

Good evening ladies and gentlemen.
Oh yeah!
Now shoot that star right outta the blue
With a right'n'a left and do-si-do.
Turn on the left and corner on the right
Back to the right and allemande

When ya meet your partner,
you're gonna promenade
Go two by two
Take a little walk all the way round
And when you get through...

7:03 pm

FIRST FIG

My candle burns at both ends;
  It will not last the night;
But, ah, my foes, and, oh my friends—
  It gives a lovely light!

—Edna St. Vincent Millay

Paul Beatty

A Three Point Shot From

rain rusted orange
ring of saturn
in urban orbit
over an outdoor gym

nighttime jumpers
pull up to the hoop
dance on the rim
bolted against a
metal backboard sky
riddled with

ninety-nine thousand
BB-sized holes
compressing fifth floor duplex
kitchen light
into a galaxy
of 50 watt schoolyard stars

supra-flex intense constellations
handcheck
rotate on defense
double down
tryin to guard
spinning playground
planetarium delirium
of black gods flyin
on neighborhood rep
shake n bake
pump fake
jab step
past orion
walk on air
and burst a reverse

Andromeda

on the stellar bear

A girl on the stairs listens to her father
Beat up her mother.
Doors bang.
She comes down in her nightgown.

The piano stands there in the dark
Like a boy with an orchid.

C. D. Wright

She plays what she can
Then turns the lamp on.

Her mother's music is spread out
On the floor like brochures.

She hears her father
Running through the leaves.

The last black key
She presses stays down, makes no sound,
Someone putting their tongue where their tooth had been

His neck was stiff
from watching the street
for men
who'd buy him.

I came by around
4 a.m. "No luck?"
"It's been slow
all night," he said.

ghosts

I couldn't see why.
He was blond
and maybe twenty
with eyes you would steal.

Not like the ghosts
on most corners,—
guys so bored
they beg to be beaten.

I'd have bought him
but he needed
more than I had
for less than I wanted.

Dennis Cooper

on most corners

We stood all night
approached by no one,
while creeps were
snatched up like teens.

I smoked his cigarettes.
He leaned back,
and the sun crept up
on our weight and our ages,

Until cars wouldn't slow
and heads didn't turn—
we turned and walked
home, to our darkness.

Star

If, in the light of things, you fade

real, yet wanly withdrawn

to our determined and appropriate

distance, like the moon left on

all night among the leaves, may

you invisibly delight this house;

O star, doubly compassionate, who came

too soon for twilight, too late

for dawn, may your pale flame

direct the worst in us

through chaos

with the passion of

plain day.

Derek Walcott

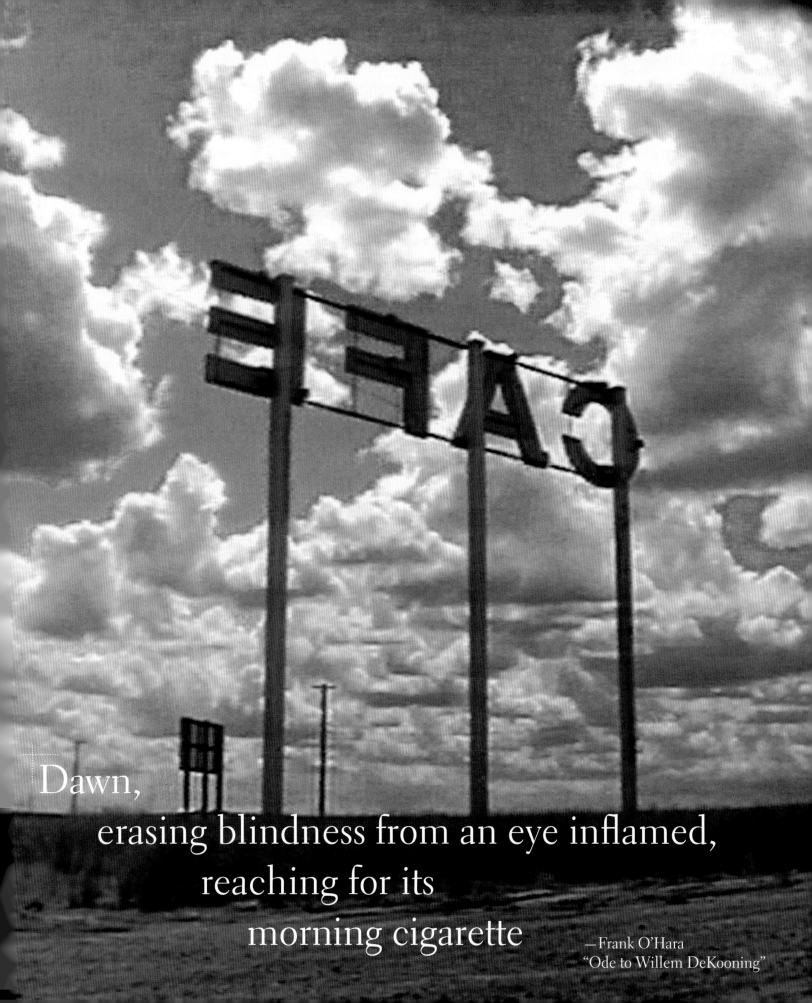

Dawn,
    erasing blindness from an eye inflamed,
    reaching for its
        morning cigarette

—Frank O'Hara
"Ode to Willem DeKooning"

Show Three

The great argument: is a poem inherently political? or does a poem with political intent cease to be a poem, become rhetoric? In The American Dream, language becomes a weapon, a stiletto of meaning to pierce the nonsensical rhetoric of politics, to unmask the cynical grab of advertising. Here, naked but knowing, words demand. Poetry has traditionally been the locus for Those Who Have Not Been Heard to speak, but who's been listening? What if the poem could be heard, what if the single voice were suddenly powerful, not as a literary conceit, but as an actual tool for building a new society, a tool for a new patriotism? Not as a speaker's corner for the powerless loyal opposition, but as creator and visionary? And if the poem were to become such a tool, wouldn't this obviate its imaginative power, its anti-utilitarian purpose as the site where one can go to get away from the world's madness? Can we live in a poem? Can a poem change the world? Now comes the redefinition of our nation. Because the poets will not answer the questions, but ask them, and it is we, the readers, who are charged, not with the passivity that TV has seemed to engender, but with a new activism. Welcome to the land not only where words say what they mean, but where the poets mean what they say.

The American Dream

POETS
We relish a
new patriotism,
symbolized by the
immigrant status of Miss
(or Ms.) Liberty herself as
heard through the words of
THYLIAS MOSS of Ann Arbor....
Cult rocker, hero to many, perhaps the
continent's most successful poet, **LEONARD COHEN** wrote the songs "Suzanne" and "Bird on a
Wire," and novels *Beautiful Losers* and *The Dangerous Game.* His poem "Democracy" can be found
on his album *The Future*....**AMIRI BARAKA**, the Father of Contemporary Black Literature, has been a force for change since his early days
as Beat poet LeRoi Jones. A brilliant critic, essayist, and music scholar, Baraka is also a transcendent live performer. He lives in Newark
with his wife, the poet Amina Baraka, and their children....Many Seattle children have learned their poetry at **EL CENTRO DE LA
RAZA**, where Director Roy Wilson follows the precepts of Nicaraguan poet Ernesto Cardenal. **NERISSA DIAZ** was eleven
years old when she wrote "Face to Face."...Born in Baton Rouge, raised in Texas, **JOHN WRIGHT** has howled his poems
from mountains but rarely been published outside of some small-press rags. He was the editor of *Bombay Gin*, the
lit-zine of the Naropa Institute. A landscaper by trade, he translates Gaelic and Celtic poetry....Rancher, truck
driver, philosopher, and poet, **VESS QUINLAN** is one of the few cowboys to actually have done time at
writing workshops and is much respected by critics of all stripes. He lives in Alamosa, Colorado, and
has successfully handed over his ranching operations to his family. His daughter, Lisa, is also a
poet....**GENNY LIM**, a professor at New College, often performs with music, tours, still
finds time to raise her two daughters, be the inspiration of a million poems, and live
where art and life collide joyfully and daily....**RUTH FORMAN** won the Barnard Poetry
Prize in 1993. A filmmaker as well as a poet, she lives in L.A....**JIM NORTHRUP** writes
a syndicated column, "The Fond Du Lac Follies," describing life on and about the Rez of
the same name in northern Minnesota where he, his wife, Patricia (who is not a poet!), and
their family live in the traditional way of the Chippewa, including making the most beautiful
rice baskets for the wild rice harvest....**LUÍS ALFARO** is a young gay Chicano loudmouth who
writes hilarious performance poems which he shouts, while dressed in a cheap, short, black lace slip,
at all the gods and people wandering the streets. He has taken his solo act around the country; he grew
up around the corner from where his poem, "Orphan of Aztlan," was shot in the Los Angeles barrio...."The
High Priestess of Word" is how **WANDA COLEMAN** is often introduced. She is a regular columnist for *The Los
Angeles Times Magazine* and, with her husband, the poet Austin Strauss, broadcasts the weekly radio show "The
Poetry Connexion" on KPFA. A mesmerizing performer, her trances entrance.... **JAVIER PIÑA** developed his poem
in a workshop at Seattle's El Centro de la Raza led by poet Zoe Angelsey....**ROBERT CHAMBERS** is a poet and activist
who has turned his knots of language into a rescue
line: "formerly homeless," he now lives in an SRO
in downtown L.A. He is actively involved
with the Los Angeles Homeless Writers'
Coalition, and edits and publishes
their newsletter....**LAWRENCE
FERLINGHETTI** is a poet,
painter, and co-founder of
San Francisco's City
Lights Publishers
and City Lights
Books.
...

Green Light and Gamma Ways

Miss Liberty is green, the horizon and sky
plus yellow skin.

She is a minority too, color
of ridiculous Martian fable
and not a man.

Handicapped, disabled.
Another immigrant.

Thylias Moss

In dreams begin responsibilities

–Delmore Schwartz

DEMOCRACY

It's coming through a hole in the air,

from those nights in Tiananmen Square.

It's coming from the feel

that it ain't exactly real,

or it's real, but it ain't exactly there.

From the wars against disorder,

from the sirens night and day;

from the fires of the homeless,

from the ashes of the gay:

Democracy is coming to the U.S.A.

It's coming through a crack in the wall,

on a visionary flood of alcohol;

from the staggering account

of the Sermon on the Mount

which I don't pretend to understand at all.

It's coming from the silence

on the dock of the bay,

from the brave, the bold, the battered

heart of Chevrolet:

Democracy is coming to the U.S.A.

It's coming from the sorrow on the street,

the holy places where the races meet;

from the homicidal bitchin'

that goes down in every kitchen

to determine who will serve and who will eat.

From the wells of disappointment

where the women kneel to pray

for the grace of G-d in the desert here

and desert far away:

Democracy is coming to the U.S.A.

Sail on, sail on

o mighty Ship of State!

To the Shores of Need

past the Reefs of Greed

through the Squalls of Hate

Sail on, sail on

It's coming to America first,

the cradle of the best and of the worst.

It's here they got the range

and the machinery for change

and it's here they got the spiritual thirst.

It's here the family's broken

and it's here the lonely say

that the heart has got to open

in a fundamental way:

Democracy is coming to the U.S.A.

It's coming from the women and the men.

O baby, we'll be making love again.

We'll be going down so deep

that the river's going to weep,

and the mountain's going to shout Amen!

It's coming like the tidal flood

beneath the lunar sway,

imperial, mysterious,

in amorous array:

Democracy is coming to the U.S.A.

Sail on, sail on

o mighty Ship of State!

To the Shores of Need

past the Reefs of Greed

through the Squalls of Hate

Sail on, sail on

I'm sentimental, if you know what I mean:

I love the country but I can't stand the scene.

And I'm neither left or right

I'm just staying home tonight,

getting lost in that hopeless little screen.

But I'm stubborn as those garbage bags

that Time cannot decay,

I'm junk but I'm still holding up

this little wild bouquet:

Democracy is coming to the U.S.A.

Leonard Cohen

The X Is Black

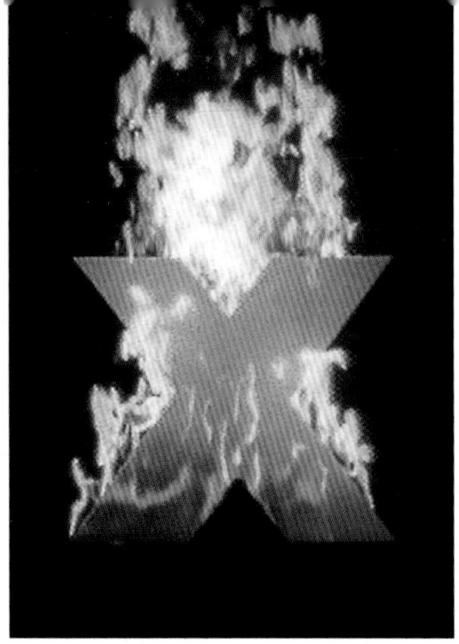

(Spike Lie)

If the flag catch
    fire, & an X
    burn in, that X is Black
    & leaves an
    empty space. It
    is that place
    where we live
    the Afro American
    Nation.

If the flag
    catch afire
    & an X burn in
    the only stripes is
    on our back
    the only star
    blown free
    in the northern sky
    no red but our
    blood, no white
    but slavers and Klux in robes
    no blue
    but our songs

If the flag catch fire
    & an X
    burn in

that X is black
& the space that is left
is our history
now a mystery

we only live
where the flag
is not
where the air is funky
the music
hot
Inside the hole
in the American soul
that space, that place
empty of democracy
we live
inside the burned boundaries
of a wasted symbol
X humans, X slaves, unknown, incorrect
crossed out, multiplying the wealth of others

If the flag
catch fire
& an X burn in
that X
believe me,
is black.

Amiri Baraka

Face to Face

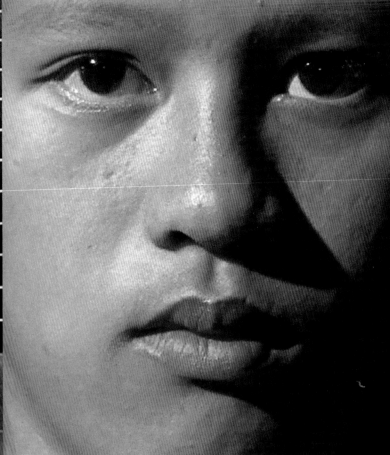

The very first time I went to the fountain
  to get a drink
    somebody pushed me in the back.
The water went up my nose.

I cried a little bit and ran to the office
  to tell the principal who was not there.
    I found a teacher
and he told the boy not to push me again.

Lunch recess the boy pushed me in the play court.
  It scared me.
    I looked at him in the face
and I said my name is Nerissa.
      Don't push me.
        I want to be your friend.

NERISSA DIAZ

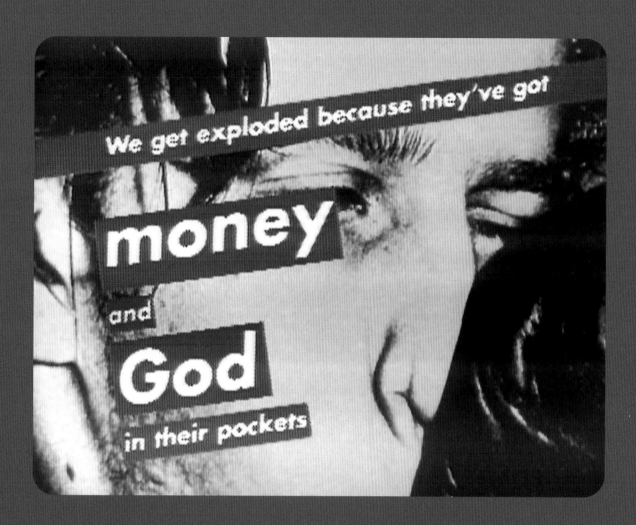

Boulder Valley Surprise

boil igneous rock for millions of years
let stand until cool
when vast inland seas subside
uplift red sandstone, crimp edges
grind soil with glaciers
boil off glaciers
decorate with trees, evergreen and deciduous
then add large mammals, fish and birds
transfer humans with stone weapons
across the Bering Strait
convert large mammals
into food clothing and shelter
then add other humans from the east
sprinkle liberally with iron and gunpowder
in a large well-wooded valley
sift for gold dust
construct wooden buildings, then add brick
steam railroads, a shot of whiskey
then, with a large spatula
smooth out even layers of concrete
on any possible surface
saute in carbon monoxide
bake with electromagnetic waves until saturated
in a large sealed container
cook plutonium until doomsday
garnish with shopping malls, tanning salons
virtual reality arcades and crystal emporia
set blender on puree
bring to a boil
run from the kitchen

John Wright

Sold Out

The worst will come tomorrow
When we load the saddle horses.
We arc past turning back;
The horses must be sold.

    The old man turns away, hurting,
    As the last cow is loaded.
    I hunt words to ease his pain
    But there is nothing to say.

        He walks away to lean
        On a top rail of the corral
        And look across the calving pasture
        Toward the willow-grown creek.

            I follow,
            Absently mimicking his walk,
            And stand a post away.
            We don't speak of causes or reasons,

                Don't speak at all;
                We just stand there
                Leaning on the weathered poles,
                While shadows consume the pasture.

Vess Quinlan

NO BITTERNESS: OUR ANCESTORS DID IT.

—Robinson Jeffers
"Ave Caesar"

Winter Place
Genny Lim

We are this hungry spool of a fishhole alley
Every night there's a derelict dog, mangy with a cataract stare
Licking the shards of old North Beach
Leftover fish 'n chips, upchucked cheesesteak, antipasti
Etched against the antiseptic glare of trendy restaurants,
Flossy Gelatos
Where MTV couples glide frozenly by
Catching in the corners of their ray-banned eyes
Their store-bought reflections

It ain't so bad
Sundry hookers straining their fleshbait
out of windows, doorways
Orifices of the Europa glistening like fish
It ain't so bad
The winos and the refugees, the bag ladies and panhandlers
Eye-talians, Chinamen, tourists, punks, junkies
Boat people and runaways
Converging on this teeming waterhole
where the corporate buffalo roams

The city reeks of crab shells, fishheads, cabbages
Soiled pampers, cappuccino and Kotex
in shocking orange-and-pink
Day-glo shopping bags ripped and spewing out the
Guts of Chinatown, Chinatown, where the lights are low
They all come
The natives like homing pigeons
Midwesterners like homesteaders
Southerners like shipwrecked sailors
Eastcoasters like fugitives
Through the fog-laden cable cars plummeting
over Russian Hill backyards and
narrow chopstick alleyways
where camera-toting tourists
eat cheap chop-suey and
snap moon-faced babies wide-eyed on their mothers' backs
out of curiosity
It ain't so bad
the Indians once said as
they traded their land for horses
as they traded their land for water
as they traded their land for beads

It ain't so bad
the Coolies reasoned
as they jumped ship only to
sweat in baskets
with pickaxes and dynamite
twenty-thousand feet in the Sierras
like wet human laundry

Stoplight Politics

check out
sista
on de corner
bar-b-q Fritos Fanta soda
dookie braids
knee-high boots
Raiders jacket
gold tooth
talkin shit

she embarrass you huh

go head sista
roll on by
you
rollin somewhere
you
gon conquer the nation
worl in yo hand
wich yo education

you
better den sista
on de corner
thank god
you never did hang wit de brothas
goin nowhere
talkin shit
waitin for de light to turn green

go head
turn yo head
look straight ahead
n roll that Lexus home
to yo fifty g man hundred g crib

pray for de light ta turn green
befo you look back ova
one more time
n realize
you both de same thang
hopin on de same thang

you jus got a car

Survived the war, but was

having trouble surviving

the peace, couldn't sleep

more than two hours

was scared to be

without a gun.

Nightmares, daymares

guilt and remorse

wanted to stay drunk

all the time.

1966 and the V.A. said

Vietnam wasn't a war.

They couldn't help, but

did give me a copy of

the yellow pages.

Picked a shrink off

the list. 50 bucks an

hour, I was making 125

a week. Spent six

sessions establishing

rapport, heard about his

military life,

his homosexuality,

his fights with his mother

and anything else he wanted

to talk about.

At this rate, we would have

got to me in 1999.

Gave up on that shrink

couldn't afford him and he

wasn't doing me any good.

Six weeks later my shrink

killed himself. Great.

Not only guilt about the

war but new guilt about

my dead shrink.

If only I had a better job,

I could have kept on

seeing him.

I thought we were making

real progress, maybe in another

six sessions, I could have

helped him.

I realized then that surviving

the peace was up to me.

Jim Northrup

ORPHAN OF AZTLAN

I am fast forwarding
past the reruns *ése*
and riding the big wave
called future
making myself
fabulous
as I disentangle
from the wreck of this
cultural collision

I am a Queer Chicano
A native in no-land
An orphan of Aztlan
The Pocho son of farm-worker parents

The Mexicans only want me
when I talk about Mexico
*But what about
Mexican Queers in L.A.?*

The Queers only want me,
when they need
to add color
add spice
like *salsa picante*,
on the side

With one foot on
each side of the border,
not the border between
México and the United States,
but the border between
Chicano and Queer,
I search for a
home in both
yet neither one
believes that
I exist

Blur the line
take the journey
play with the unknown
deal with the whole *enchilada*

We will continue
to create these
espectáculos tan sabrosos
that we can call our Queer Latino selves
and we will make them
al estilo los
like only we know
how to make them
Because we are
at the edge
at the rim
at the border
of a new world
and there is no place
to run
or hide

So tonight

I walk down
to the corner
I step over
this burned out lot
and say
I come in the name of peace and justice
and I ask
What are you afraid of?

Are you a
friend
or a
phobe?

Luís Alfaro

i need to talk hard cash

how it fuels passion

how to make it user friendly

Talk About the Money

i need to talk hard cash. how to make it work
how to not be afraid of it. how to make it user friendly
how to plant it and make it sprout or tame
it cage it and admire its ferocious beauty
(all the more beautiful for being in my capture)
how to satisfy it and in return, have it satisfy

i need to talk serious money. how it fuels passion
how it endows with power. how and what insufficient
quantities of it aborts. we need to talk money. to
understand the current currency of our time. what it
means to survive in this new dawn of the whore

we cannot afford to be naive. ignorance and being
sincere solve nothing. we need to speak coin
to establish credit. to lift ourselves
by our own purse-straps

we need to be able to bank on each other

to live life in the black

Wanda Coleman

how to satisfy it and in return, have it satisfy

Bilingual in a Cardboard Box

Soy Mexicano
I'm an American

Puedo cantar canciones del corazón
I am mute

Puedo ver los colores de la puesta del sol
I am blind

Puedo escuchar las voces de los pajaritos cantando
I am deaf

Soy indígena bailando al cielo que llora
I'm forever seated in a chair with wheels

Todos me respetan
I'm labeled by pointing fingers

Tengo mucho dinero
I live in a cardboard box

Estoy riéndome con el mundo alegre
I am sad

Salgo con mis amigos
I am alone

Estoy soñando
and I don't want to wake up!

Javier Piña
El Centro de la Raza

Robert Chambers

Tumbling
(Through the Safety Net of the American Economy)

Tumbling
Tumbling

Tumbling through the Safety Net into the black void

Tumbling

Tumbling in the vortex, stressed, compressed by 250 million
G's of indifference

Crush
Crushed

Tumbling
Tumbling

Tumbling like lint, spin dried in a circumscripted orbit
too near the Sun

Tumbling

Tumbling till you're ripped apart by the stress, dissected,
circumfluent till the only thing that trickles down is your
blood

Pain
Pained

Tumbling
Tumbling

Tumbling till you face yourself again, juxtaposed, then
circumjacent in Einstein's trick of time

Tumbling till you're disintegrated watching yourself
miraculously a molecular breakdown, a beam excellerated, yet
each atom that is

Spinning
Spinning

Is still you

Tumbling
Tumbling

Tumbling like Love through the rich man's fingers
Tumbling like Hope through the poor man's heart

Tumbling
Tumbling

Tumbling like the circumflexions of a scream

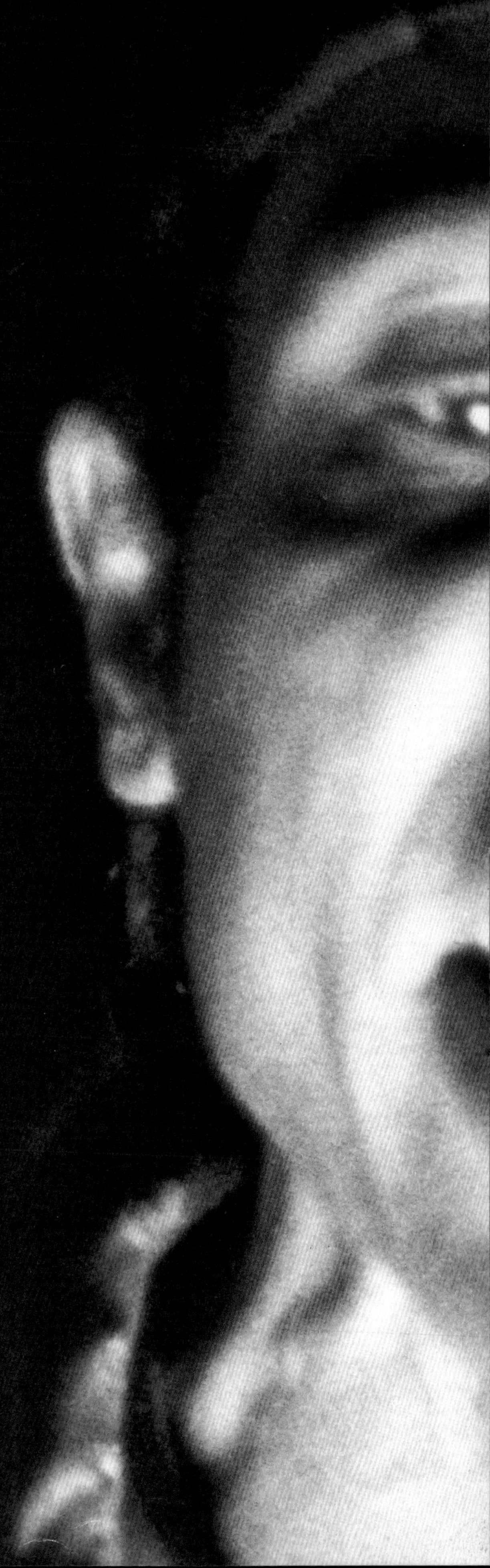

Remember
Me

I am waiting for my case to come up
and I am waiting
for a rebirth of wonder
and I am waiting for someone
to really discover America
and wail
and I am waiting
for the discovery
of a new symbolic western frontier
and I am waiting
for the American Eagle
to really spread its wings
and straighten up and fly right
and I am waiting
for the Age of Anxiety
to drop dead
and I am waiting
for the war to be fought
which will make the world safe
for anarchy
and I am waiting
for the final withering away
of all governments
and I am perpetually awaiting
a rebirth of wonder

I am waiting for the Second Coming
and I am waiting
for a religious revival
to sweep thru the state of Arizona
and I am waiting
for the Grapes of Wrath to be stored
and I am waiting
for them to prove
that God is really American
and I am waiting
to see God on television
piped onto church altars
if only they can find
the right channel
to tune in on
and I am waiting
for the Last Supper to be served again
with a strange new appetizer
and I am perpetually awaiting
a rebirth of wonder

I am waiting

I am waiting for my number to be called
and I am waiting
for the Salvation Army to take over
and I am waiting
for the meek to be blessed
and inherit the earth
without taxes
and I am waiting
for forests and animals
to reclaim the earth as theirs
and I am waiting
for a way to be devised
to destroy all nationalisms
without killing anybody
and I am waiting
for linnets and planets to fall like rain
and I am waiting for lovers and weepers
to lie down together again
in a new rebirth of wonder

I am waiting for the Great Divide to be crossed
and I am anxiously waiting
for the secret of eternal life to be discovered
by an obscure general practitioner
and I am waiting
for the storms of life
to be over
and I am waiting
to set sail for happiness
and I am waiting
for a reconstructed Mayflower
to reach America
with its picture story and tv rights
sold in advance to the natives
and I am waiting
for the lost music to sound again
in the Lost Continent
in a new rebirth of wonder

I am waiting for the day
that maketh all things clear
and I am awaiting retribution
for what America did
to Tom Sawyer
and I am waiting
for Alice in Wonderland
to retransmit to me
her total dream of innocence
and I am waiting
for Childe Roland to come
to the final darkest tower
and I am waiting
for Aphrodite
to grow live arms
at a final disarmament conference
in a new rebirth of wonder

I am waiting
to get some intimations
of immortality
by recollecting my early childhood
and I am waiting
for the green mornings to come again
youth's dumb green fields come back again
and I am waiting
for some strains of unpremeditated art
to shake my typewriter
and I am waiting to write
the great indelible poem
and I am waiting
for the last long careless rapture
and I am perpetually waiting
for the fleeing lovers on the Grecian Urn
to catch each other up at last
and embrace
and I am awaiting
perpetually and forever
a renaissance of wonder

Lawrence Ferlinghetti

Show Four

Who wrote "Who Wrote the Book of Love?"? Poets. The domain of the heart, struggling to twin, that's where the poet and the poem step in. Here's the place where everybody's words climb to the sublime — or try to. And who's to say? Why, the Beloved of course! Even the purists seem not to object to poetry's being put to the utilitarian purpose of Cupid's heart dart! Of course this does open up a fairly large topic for discussion, namely, ahem, What is love? Passion, lust, sex, and crushed velvet nighties...love for children and for parents...the search for a balanced co-peer un-co-dependency? Love of country and health foods, love of art and of the great outdoors, of God and country — love, love, love! Here we'd best let the poets speak for themselves....

Love and Sex

THE POETS

PEARL CLEAGE is considered the Poet Laureate of Atlanta. She is part of a new movement of African American women writers who speak direct and carry a big agenda, rooted in the things of life, not rhetoric. The author of five books, she was filmed for USOP with her husband, playwright Zaron W. Burnett, Jr., on their honeymoon in Memphis....A ranch in Recluse, Wyoming, is the backdrop for **SUE WALLIS**'s love poem, "Timothy Draw." Widely regarded as one of the finest of the new cowboy versifiers (and purveyor of the sentiment that "Women can be cowboy poets, too!"), Sue grew up in Recluse and now lives in Ruby Valley, Nevada, where she tends to the herd and her husband, the poet Rod McQueary, as well as the Western Folklife Center's annual Cowboy Poetry Gathering in Elko, Nevada....An original Beat, co-founder with Anne Waldman of the Jack Kerouac School of Disembodied Poetics in Boulder, **ALLEN GINSBERG** died April 8, 1997. Rest in Poetry....Surely **MAGGIE ESTEP** had more of a reason to become a poet than simply "I get to say cheese a lot." But, alas, that is what she says. Her poems slide slyly into rock 'n' roll, her intelligent takes give good beat, and attitude! First album: *No More Mr. Nice Girl* with her band, I Love Everybody (NuYo/Imago Records)....A native of Sri Lanka, **INDRAN AMIRTHANAYAGAM** is following in his father's footsteps by being both a poet and a U.S. Foreign Service officer; he is currently on assignment to Argentina....**JOHN S. HALL** is a pioneer of the new Spoken Word Movement. He has toured individually, with band (currently all celli, The Body Has a Head) for MTV, and as a furniture mover. He has released seven albums (most recently *King Missile* on Atlantic Records), and had a #1 hit on college radio with the indefensible "Detachable Penis."...Professor, poet, biographer (of Miles Davis), anthologist, **QUINCY TROUPE** is one of our country's finest jazz poets. Son of a catcher in the Negro Leagues, currently head of the Writing Department at University of California at San Diego, he appears in USOP with his wife, Margaret, who is also a poet, and a stand-in for their son Porter, who outgrew the part....His poem "Romeo Had Juliette" can be found on his quintessential rock portrait, *New York*. **LOU REED** is the Man who not only walks on the wild side but wrote the song about it. His most recent record is *Magic and Loss*; from the Velvet Underground till now, no one has done more for the poetic beat than Lou.... Nobel Prize-winning poet **JOSEPH BRODSKY** made his last television appearance in USOP. He died shortly after the series premiere in 1996, having just finished his tenure as Poet Laureate. Wish you were here, dear....**MIGUEL ALGARÍN** is the founder of the Nuyorican Poets Café and Professor of Shakespeare at Rutgers University. His life and work span the academy and the street. Of his seven books, three are bilingual and one, *Time's Now/Ya Es Tiempo*, recently went trilingual when published in Tokyo. He is co-editor with Bob Holman of *ALOUD! Voices from the Nuyorican Poets Café*....**SANDRA CISNEROS** has won numerous awards, including a MacArthur Fellowship, has seen her work translated into ten languages, and currently lives in San Antonio, where she is nobody's mother and nobody's wife....Who is that elegant creature in the fancy chapeau and heels, strolling down Fifth Avenue to introduce us to Love? Internationally renowned lipsyncher **LYPSINKA**, that's who! Here she mouths the lines of Elizabeth Barrett Browning, as originally voiced by actress Jayne Mansfield....

Turning Forty

Pearl Cleage

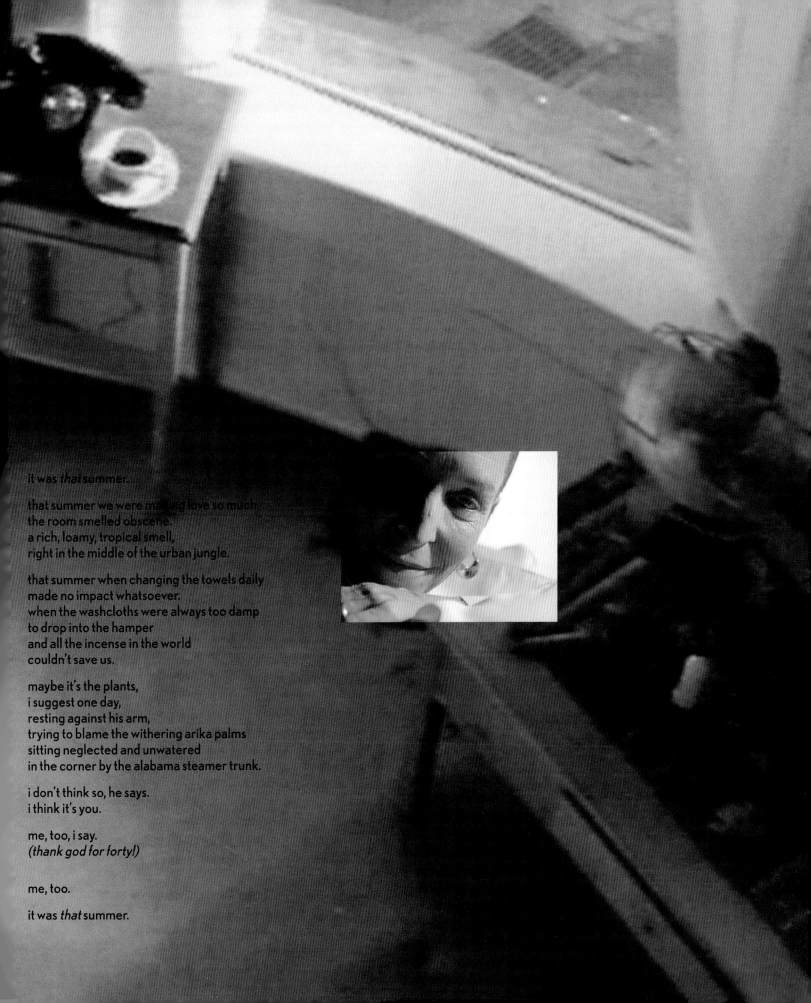

it was *that* summer.

that summer we were making love so much
the room smelled obscene.
a rich, loamy, tropical smell,
right in the middle of the urban jungle.

that summer when changing the towels daily
made no impact whatsoever.
when the washcloths were always too damp
to drop into the hamper
and all the incense in the world
couldn't save us.

maybe it's the plants,
i suggest one day,
resting against his arm,
trying to blame the withering arika palms
sitting neglected and unwatered
in the corner by the alabama steamer trunk.

i don't think so, he says.
i think it's you.

me, too, i say.
(thank god for forty!)

me, too.

it was *that* summer.

It is the happy heart that breaks

—Sara Teasdale
"What Do I Care"

Timothy Draw

Sue Wallis

We pause at the top of Timothy Draw
Look down the country for stray cows
He cocks his head
Stands in the stirrups
Hands on the horn
Relaxed and easy and graceful
He moves with a horse
Like few men can

In one brief, quick space
I love him more
Than I will ever love again

Like passion, but not of sex
Like Life without death
Like the nudge and the tug and the sleepy smile
Of a too-full child at your still-full breast
Something that explodes from your toes
But flows through your bones
Like warm honey

More powerful than violence

I lift my reins
Our horses sidestep
...and we slip on down the draw

Personals Ad

Poet professor in autumn years
 seeks helpmate companion protector friend
 young lover w/empty compassionate soul
 exuberant spirit, straightforward handsome
 athletic physique & boundless mind, courageous
 warrior who may also like women & girls, no problem,
 to share bed meditation apartment Lower East Side,
 help inspire mankind conquer world anger & guilt,
 empowered by Whitman Blake Rimbaud Ma Rainey & Vivaldi,
 familiar respecting Art's primordial majesty, priapic carefree
 playful harmless slave or master, mortally tender passing swift time,
 photographer, musician, painter, poet, yuppie or scholar—
 Find me here in New York alone with the Alone
 going to lady psychiatrist who says Make time in your life
 for someone you can call darling, honey, who holds you dear
 can get excited & lay his head on your heart in peace.

I'm an Emotional Idiot So Get Away from Me

I'm an emotional idiot
so get away from me.
I mean, come here.

Wait, no,
that's <u>too</u> close,
give me some space
it's a big country,
there's plenty of room,
don't sit so close to me.

Hey, where are you?
I haven't seen you in days.
Whadya, having an affair?
Who is she?
Come on,
aren't I enough for you?

God,
You're so cold.
I never know what you're thinking.
You're not very affectionate.

I mean,
you're clinging to me,
DON'T TOUCH ME,
what am I, your fucking cat?
Don't rub me like that.

Don't you have anything better to do
than sit there fawning over me?

Don't you have any interests?
Hobbies?
Sailing
Fly fishing
Archeology?

There's an archeology expedition leaving tomorrow

why don't you go?

I'll loan you the money,

my money is your money.
My life is your life
my soul is yours
without you I'm nothing.

Move in with me
we'll get a studio apartment together, save on rent,
well, wait, I mean, a one bedroom,
so we don't get in each other's hair or anything
or, well,
maybe a two bedroom
I'll have my own bedroom,
it's nothing personal
I just need to be alone sometimes,
you do understand,
don't you?

Hey, why are you acting distant?

Where you going
Was it something I said?
What
What did I do?

I'm an emotional idiot
so get away from me.

I mean,

MARRY ME.

Maggie Estep

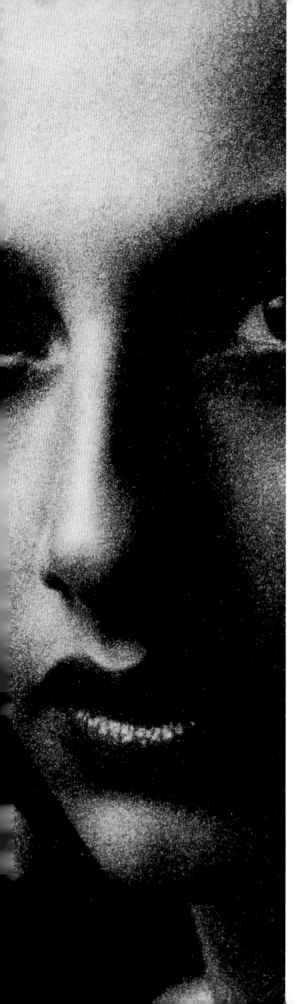

So Beautiful

So beautiful that couple
in handsome black and red clothes
walking along the street
her arms folded, his in pockets cold...
Scarves loosely wrapped about white necks,

And in the subway car
a black man takes a black woman's hands,
and her eyes look far away
beyond the walls under the sea,

and his eyes concentrate on her hands
as glasses drop slightly down his nose
as she turns and smiles, as he looks up
at clay made whole,

and she takes her hands about his cheeks
makes a vase, and he smiles
as roses are put in his mouth and hair,

and her brown leather coat crumples
as she kisses him,
and his black windbreaker is crumpled
by her kiss,

And for two subway stops their kiss
moves a man to write
and get up in the morning
and sing an old song

to remember a woman in a dream
who held his hands
wearing ear rings of white moons,
in black hair open as a fan,

blowing honeyed wind about the room
in which they loved and loved,
as kingdoms came and went,
in which they loved and loved

as the black man and woman
left their embrace
to slowly get up to the door
by an old man in the window seat
into whose hands dropped two white moons.

Indran Amirthanayagam

My Lover

John S. Hall

I find it
Particularly enjoyable
When my lover
Drips
Hot candlewax
On my nipples

Light the wick, lover
And drip
The wax
On my nipples

Do it
I find it enjoyable

Change

For Margaret & Porter

use to be eye would be lying there
in margaret's lap, longside her sweet
soft thighs, on sunday mornings, sipping
champagne, sucking on her soft, open lips
drinking in the love from her moist, brown eyes
now, porter's there, giggling, twenty month old
squirming squeals—a tiny, spitting image of me—
his eyes kissing everyone, including me, & me?
well, yall, eye'm sitting here, apart from them
hungry, alone, in my favorite chair
watching television
& watching them, watching me

Quincy Troupe

113

Romeo Had Juliet

Caught between the twisted stars the plotted lines the faulty map

that brought Columbus to New York

Betwixt between the east and west

he calls on her wearing a leather vest

the earth squeals and shudders to a halt

A diamond crucifix in his ear is used to help ward off the fear

that he has left his soul in someone's rented car

Inside his pants he hides a mop

to clean the mess that he has dropped

into the life of lithesome Juliette Bell

And Romeo wanted Juliette

and Juliette wanted Romeo

Romeo Rodriguez squares his shoulders and curses Jesus

runs a comb through his black pony-tail

He's thinking of his lonely room

The sink that by his bed gives off a stink

then smells her perfume in his eyes

and her voice was like a bell

Outside the streets were steaming the crack dealers were dreaming

of an Uzi someone had just scored

I betcha I could hit that light

with my one good arm behind my back

says little Joey Diaz

Brother, give me another tote

those downtown hoods are no damn good

Those Italians need a lesson to be taught

This cop who died in Harlem you think they'd get the warnin'

I was dancing when his brains ran out on the street

and Romeo had Juliette

and Juliette had her Romeo

I'll take Manhattan in a garbage bag

with Latin writ on it that says

"It's hard to give a shit these days"*

Manhattan's sinking like a rock, into the filthy Hudson

what a shock

They wrote a book about it, they said it was like Ancient Rome

The perfume burned his eyes, holding tightly to her thighs

and something flickered for a minute

and then it vanished and was gone

       Lou Reed

*ASPERUM AESTIMARE FIMI ALIQUID HODIE

A Song

I wish you were here, dear,
I wish you were here.
I wish you sat on the sofa
and I sat near.
The handkerchief could be yours,
the tear could be mine, chin-bound.
Though it could be, of course,
the other way around.

I wish you were here, dear,
I wish you were here.
I wish we were in my car,
and you'd shift the gear.
We'd find ourselves elsewhere,
on an unknown shore.
Or else we'd repair
to where we've been before.

I wish you were here, dear,
I wish you were here.
I wish I knew no astronomy
when stars appear,
when the moon skims the water
that sighs and shifts in its slumber.
I wish it were still a quarter
to dial your number.

I wish you were here, dear,
in this hemisphere,
as I sit on the porch
sipping a beer.
It's evening; the sun is setting,
boys shout and gulls are crying.
What's the point of forgetting
if it's followed by dying?

Joseph Brodsky

Quarantine

Sometimes I fear touching your plump ear lobes,
I might contaminate you.
Sometimes I refuse odors that would
drive my hands to open your thick thighs,
sometimes closing my ears to your
voice wrenches my stomach
and I vomit to calm wanting.
Can it be that I am the bearer of plagues?
Am I poison to desire?
Do I have to deny yearning for firm full flesh
so that I'll not kill what I love?
No juices can flow 'tween you and me,
only dry sands
will suck me in.

Miguel Algarín

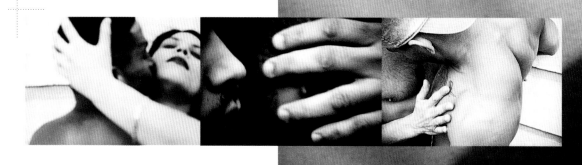

Lover to lover, no kiss,
no touch, but forever and ever this.

—H.D.
"At Baia"

I *Am* on My *Way* to Oklahoma to Bury the Man I Nearly Left
My Husband For

Your name doesn't matter.
I loved you.
We loved.
The years

I waited
by the river for your pickup
truck to find me. Footprints
scattered in the yellow sand.
Husband, mother-
in-law, kids wondering
where I'd gone.

You wouldn't
the years I begged. Would
the years I wouldn't. Only
one of us had sense at a time.

I won't see you again.
I guess life presents you
choices and you choose. Smarter
over the years. Oh smarter.
The sensible thing smarting
over the years, the sensible
thing to excess, I guess.

My life—deed I have
done to artistic extreme—I
drag you with me. Must wake
early. Ride north tomorrow.
Send you off. Are you fine?
I think of you often, friend,
and fondly.

Sandra Cisneros

How Do I Love Thee? Let Me Count the Ways

How do I love thee? Let me count the ways.
I love thee to the depth and breadth and height
my soul can reach, when feeling out of sight
For the ends of Being, an ideal Grace.
I love thee to the level of every day's
Most quiet need; by sun and candle-light.
I love thee freely, as men strive for Right;
I love thee purely, as they turn from Praise.
I love thee with the passion put to use
In my old griefs, and with my childhood's faith.
I love thee with a love I seemed to lose
With my lost saints,—I love thee with the breath,
Smiles, tears, of all my life!—and, if God choose,
I shall but love thee better after death.

Elizabeth Barrett Browning

Sonnet XLII

SONNETS FROM THE PORTUGUESE

(read by Lypsinka)

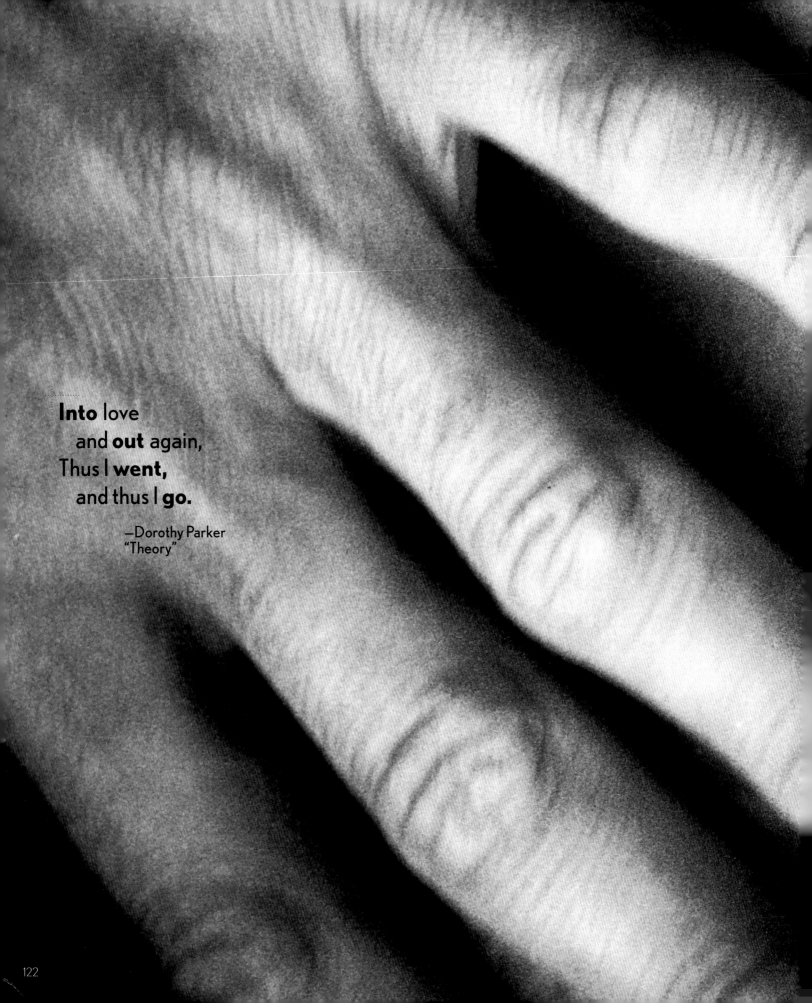

Into love
and **out** again,
Thus I **went,**
and thus I **go.**

—Dorothy Parker
"Theory"

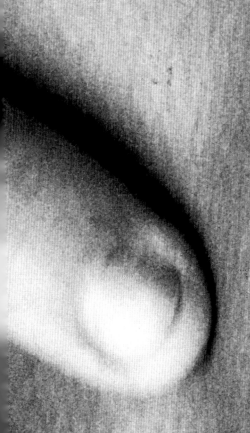

Love, ah Love, when your slipknot's drawn
We can but say, "Farewell, good sense."

—Marianne Moore
"The Lion in Love"

I am the least difficult of men. All I want is boundless love.

—Frank O'Hara
"Meditations in an Emergency"

Show Five

Poems are made of words. Theirs is a fragile architecture. Is "the apple" green? or red or yellow? Hanging on the tree or baked in the pie? Is it knowledge, the darling of your eye, or New York City? Of course, it is all the above, and more. *"In the Beginning was the Word"* says one book, as if the dawning of the intellect were the beginning of the universe. In other words—it's all words. There is an underlying playfulness in our current literary theorists, with their concepts of deconstruction (stripping old meanings away to find new, the way rappers mine old riffs for new meanings as "samples") and semiotics (where words are but the signs and symbols of things). Our poets are not theorists but artists, for whom the lush sounds of syllables add shades and deep resonance, and as they tickle our ears with meanings within meanings, the possibilities of poetry add dimensions to the act of being. May we be inspired. This is not the end. Word.

THE POETS Born and raised in Orange, California, **CARLA HARRYMAN** is a leading force in the West Coast Language poetry movement. Here the avant-garde has a deconstructed face, narrative is a character, and, in much of Carla's poetry, an erotic tension informs the work. She has written nine books and commutes with her husband, the poet Barrett Watten, and their son Asa between Berkeley and Detroit.... Considered by many to be our finest poet, **ROBERT CREELEY** has published over twenty books including his extraordinary *Collected* from the University of California in 1984. He has taught all over the world and is currently the Samuel Capen Professor of Poetry and the Humanities at SUNY Buffalo. He has been actively involved in poetics since his days at Black Mountain College, when he was editor of *The Black Mountain Review* with Charles Olson.... **WILLIE PERDOMO** is a Grand Slam Champ at the Nuyorican Poets Café and the author of *Where A Nickel Costs A Dime* (Norton). His life is all in his poems. His mama, Carmen, appears in his poem in our series. ...Teachers and Writers Collaborative in New York City originally sent poet Sheryl Noethe to Salmon, Idaho, high in the Rockies, to teach a one-shot workshop. The idea bloomed into a full-scale literacy program, with the whole town showing up for poetry readings at the Grange Hall. **SAWYER SHEFTS** has read there often. He is in the third grade, lives in Salmon, and wants to be a poet when he grows up....**RUSSELL LEONG** is the author of two books of poetry and recently received the PEN Josephine Miles Literature Award. Leong is a professor at UCLA, where he also edits *Amerasia Journal*. He is known for a subtlety and depth that stretch the mind to the inner forces of a poem, where life lives.... Right there in the semiotic deep-fry, where language meets music for a quick cocktail before hightailing it over the border to some Utopic greensward or other (useta be a city!), this is the habitat of one **MICHÉLLE T. CLINTON**, the fierce sister from L.A., now Berkeley, who lets you off the hook only when you say "I do" and go ahead and marry her poetry. Voted "One of the Best" performing poets by *High Performance Magazine*, she is the author of three books....Sitting in the control room of a radio station and smoking a cigarette is a long-haired, quiet, intense young man. The lights blink ON AIR ON AIR, and then switch to **JACK KEROUAC**. And indeed the words are from the author of *On the Road*, and here the voice breaks into "Chorus 113" of Kerouac's *Mexico City Blues*, perhaps the greatest volume of straightout jazz poetry ever written. And the man who's reading them, in a gently inflected smoke-tinged voice, is **JOHNNY DEPP**, who, when not starring in movies like *What's Eating Gilbert Grape?*, is an avid Kerouac fan and scholar....**LARRY EIGNER** was born in Swampscot, Massachusetts, in 1927; he now resides in Berkeley. Since childhood he has used a wheelchair due to cerebral palsy. He has published over thirty books since his first in 1953....At last, The United States of Poetry has its own President, **JIMMY CARTER**. His careers as politician, peace consultant, and housing activist (with Habitat) are well known. Less so may be his work as a poet—his first book of poetry was released in 1995....If you're looking for a rapper of intelligence and phat rhyme, try **MICHAEL FRANTI**, the progenitor of Alternative Rap. As the lead vocalist and writer for the bands the Beatnigs, Disposable Heroes of Hiphoprisy, and, currently, Spearhead, Franti has indeed "spearheaded" a new movement. We're proud to have the man included in The United States of Poetry, where he can pick up his props any time as leading citizen of that land where the language spoken is Poetry. A hero. Not of the disposable ilk, either. More like a cross between James Joyce and Langston Hughes kind of thing.... **EMILY XYZ** is a fixture on the New York performance and poetry scene, and her poems often go so far as to demand a second voice to carry their multilayered punch—she usually performs with actress Myers Bartlett, who appears with her in The United States of Poetry. Hailing from upstate New York, Ms. XYZ has recently released her second record (*Jimmy Page* backed with *Frank Sinatra*, from the Kill Rock Stars label) and is studying economics at Columbia in her spare time....**BESMILR BRIGHAM** was born some seventy years ago in Pace, Mississippi, and until recently lived in Horatio, Arkansas, with her husband and fifty or so cats. The winner of an NEA Fellowship and a student of Robert Duncan, Brigham published her only book, *Heaved from the Earth*, in 1971 with New Directions. She and her husband, Roy (who appears with her in our series), currently live in New Mexico with their daughter Heloise and her husband, the poet Keith Wilson....The poet **AI** lives a reclusive life with her five cats in Tempe, Arizona. Of distinctly mixed ancestry—including African, Japanese, German, and Native American—she has published five books of poetry and has received fellowships from the Guggenheim Foundation, the NEA, and Radcliffe, among others....Currently living in Chicago, **PETER COOK** is probably the most accessible poet who "writes" in American Sign Language today. Of course, for Peter the poem is composed "on" his body, and for those not skilled at Sign, this appears as an amalgam of gesture, dance, and almost-mimed theatrics. With the overlay of the (unspoken) language of the deaf, Peter's performance becomes a metaphor for The United States of Poetry: giving voice to those who have not been heard....

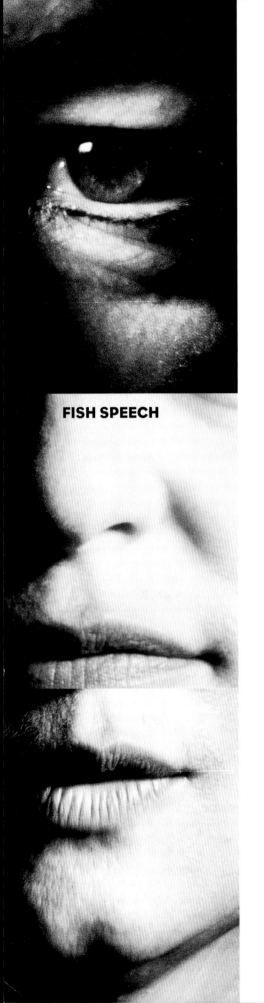

FISH SPEECH

In the beginning, there was nothing. No cattails, no wigs, no paws. There was no doom. No lavender or shirt sleeves. No burn no yellow or rest. Neither was there beginning. No light went out. No one held her own against an array of misshapen events. There were no chains. There was no writing or speech. There was nothing to shave, nothing to swim, and nothing to cut. Clouds were not clouds. Silence was neither dominant, nor peaceful, nor silent. There was no salt or smell. No twisted seaweed. Or any buoyant flowering possibility of an ambiguous growth. There were no killers and fleeting lives. There were neither chains of events nor metaphor. There were no stories or bones. No mulch or cocoons. No lizard, pelicans, or fish.

In the beginning, there were no instructions and nothing was abstract. There was nothing to identify. And no revision or modification of the description of the thing identified. Neither were there eyes nor touch. There were no millipedes. Earthworms did not nurture the soil. There was no nurturing, no soil, no worms of any kind. There was no inferno.

Sound, word, rhythm, pucker, loss, organization, and signature were nothing. There was no distance. There were no tornadoes and no change in the atmosphere. There was no atmosphere and no alteration. There was no heat, or hint of the future, no possibility of Dante. For hints, futures, possibilities did not exist. There was no extinction. There were no keys or clues. There was no DNA. Nothing squeezed. There was no singularity or multiplicity. There was no red.

In the beginning, there was nothing to hold and nothing to hold in mind. Since there was no beginning, no nothing, and no mind. The end also did not exist. Nothing stopped. There was no gender, no extremes, no image or lack of image and no money. There were no pencils. In the beginning, there were no names.

In the beginning, there was no apoliticized moment of the absolute and no political critiques. Neither was there the hibiscus flowering bearded orchid cunt juices or a male suspect. Neither black nor brown nor white. No maiming and nothing to maim. No future and nothing to preserve.

Carla Harryman

The long road...

The long road of it all
is an echo,
a sound like an image
expanding, frames growing
one after one in ascending
or descending order, all
of us a rising, falling
thought, an explosion
of emptiness soon forgotten

•

As a kid I wondered
where do they go,
my father dead. The place
had a faded dustiness
despite the woods and all.
We all grew up.
I see our faces
in old school pictures.
Where are we now?

Robert Creeley

I'm stuck
in a poem
that sounds
like the rounds
of bullets
you expect
after the sudden
screech on the
avenue.

Papo's *Ars Poetica*

I'm stuck
in a poem
like a mother's
long cry that fills
the empty
hallways and
sneaks under
my door like
the beginning of
dinner.

My eyes
are buried
in this poem
like traffic
lights peeping
last night's
rites and
passages,
painting a dog
and cat jungle
boogie chase.

Willie Perdomo

My teeth
bite on
this poem
like the wind
that chews on
tomorrow's myths
that men
are busy
making on
noontime
corners where
my ears are
stashed on
the down low:

I'm stuck
in this poem
like a squealing
rat caught on a
discount glue
trap or dead
flies floating on
fresh streams of
piss psst psst
mira mami
I'm home in
the street of
this poem where
I'm stuck.

"I heard Papo fell
off like a bad
bag of ————"

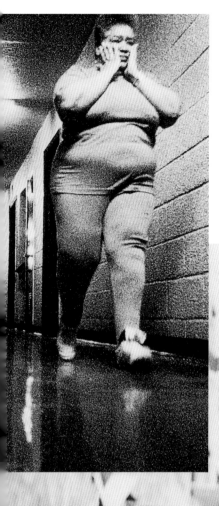

why words?

to swear + seduce + flatter + announce

to offer + predict + question + threaten

to pray + confess + declare + gossip

to slander + toast + inform + lie

to ask + answer + answer + answer

to deny + scorn + weaken + fool

to give + reveal + preach + expose

At night I hear the dog bark
The wind blows my swing

My Dad is snoring
My Mom is going like plunck, plunck
My Dad is snoring like — *Wait.*
My Dad is snoring — *Ohh. Did I get it right?*

At night I hear the dog bark
The wind blows my swing

My Dad is snoring
My Mom is going like plunck, plunck
My Dad is snoring like zzzzzzzz. *But — awwwwww*

At night I hear the dog bark
The wind blows my swing

My Dad is snoring
My brother — *Wait. Oopsie.*

At night I hear the dog bark
The wind blows my swing

My Dad is snoring
My Mom is going like plunck, plunck
My Dad is snoring like zzzzzzz, zzzzzzz

My brother is sleepwalking like ahhhh, ahhhh, ahhhhh

But I like those sounds.

OK. Can I do it again?

S O U N D S
Sawyer Shefts

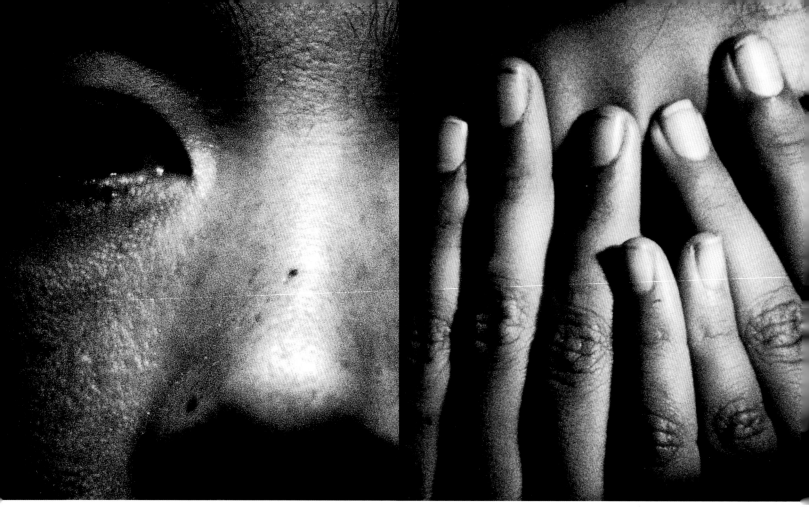

As it turns,
Every part has day
And night by turns.

As a child, a fugitive flees from me,
he who was bound to suffer
in the shadow of his body,
casually as a boy's or carefully as a girl's.

As a child, he plays hide
and seek behind the grave
thoughts of his mother and father.
Now you see him, now you don't.

As a child, he picks up odd things,
sticks and stones, and so discovers
how another's love or loneness
can desire or diminish him.

As a child, the one who awaits me
eclipses his own flesh,
frame for arm and form for thigh:
thus bound, and thus free.

Every part
Has day and night
By turns.

ECLIPSE
Russell Leong

Solitude Ain't Loneliness

Michélle
T.
Clinton

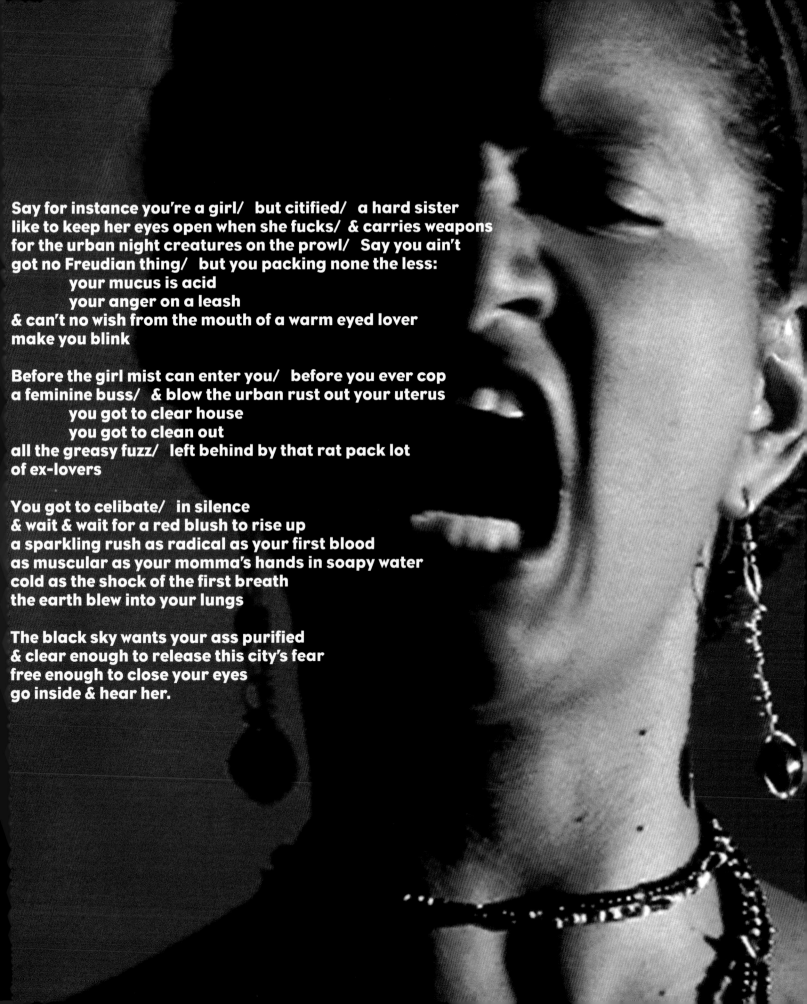

Say for instance you're a girl/ but citified/ a hard sister
like to keep her eyes open when she fucks/ & carries weapons
for the urban night creatures on the prowl/ Say you ain't
got no Freudian thing/ but you packing none the less:
         your mucus is acid
         your anger on a leash
& can't no wish from the mouth of a warm eyed lover
make you blink

Before the girl mist can enter you/ before you ever cop
a feminine buss/ & blow the urban rust out your uterus
         you got to clear house
         you got to clean out
all the greasy fuzz/ left behind by that rat pack lot
of ex-lovers

You got to celibate/ in silence
& wait & wait for a red blush to rise up
a sparkling rush as radical as your first blood
as muscular as your momma's hands in soapy water
cold as the shock of the first breath
the earth blew into your lungs

The black sky wants your ass purified
& clear enough to release this city's fear
free enough to close your eyes
go inside & hear her.

Got up and dressed up
          and went out & got laid
Then died and got buried
          in a coffin in the grave,
Man—
          Yet everything is perfect,
Because it is empty,
Because it is perfect
          with emptiness,
Because it's not even happening.

Everything
Is Ignorant of its own emptiness—
Anger
Doesn't like to be reminded of fits—

You start with the Teaching
          Inscrutable of the Diamond
And end with it, your goal
          is your startingplace,
No race was run, no walk
          of prophetic toenails
Across Arabies of hot
          meaning—you just
          numbly dont get there

—Jack **Kerouac**

(read by Johnny **Depp**)

Mexico City Blues

"Chorus **113**"

```
what time is
    it day

    I may
  sleep

  hour on hour
or all the time, what
    a consideration, you
    pretty good,
        what a question    forwards in
            a circle the
          other way around it
                  may
              have gone, the thought
                of what to do    a tree
              sits and birds come
                there's a word for each leaf, and each
                                    wall and

            a word for nothing
```

Larry Eigner

when?

words

when you found out

when the time is right

when the boat is sinking

when you are pregnant

when you're about to come

when the fever breaks

when the government falls

when your child is missing

when the sniper fires

when the farm is sold

when I am past caring

when you refuse to help me

when you cry in your sleep

when I am afraid for you

when I must know

when the end is near

when it's all over

when?

at the last possible second

Considering the Void

When I behold the charm
of evening skies, their lulling endurance;
the patterns of stars with names
of bears and dogs, a swan, a virgin;
other planets that the *Voyager* showed
were like and so unlike our own,
with all their diverse moons,
bright discs, weird rings, and cratered faces;
comets with their streaming tails
bent by pressure from our sun;
the skyscape of our Milky Way
holding in its shimmering disc
an infinity of suns
(or say a thousand billion);
knowing there are holes of darkness
gulping mass and even light,
knowing that this galaxy of ours
is one of multitudes
in what we call the heavens,
it troubles me. It troubles me.

Jimmy Carter

It is difficult
to get the news from poems
        yet men die miserably every day
                for lack
of what is found there.

—William Carlos Williams
"Asphodel, That Greeny Flower"

Sittin in the park
takin off my sneakers
had slow jams
in my headphone speakers
I just had a fight
with my best friend
and I'm not feelin alright
cause I love him
times we don't get along but we got to move on
like a funky song down a river

times we don't get along but we got to move on

make ya shiver...so ya get out of the water
go and call yo fatha...

and remember all the things
that he shoulda done for ya
and that he shoulda told ya
when he scold ya
and ya think ya probably deserved it
that's what makes ya nervous

things that should get said never get said
up inside my head up
I feel a bad set of waves comin on
and deep inside my heart I know I gotta
start cleanin up the mess that's been buildin up so long

start cleanin up the mess that's been buildin up so long

but forward ever, backward never
this is what we say when we hit the stormy weather

But Terminator smashed cops like glass
and I remember Schwarzenegger kissin Bush's ass
Bill Clinton got lipstick on the collar
everybody in the media started to holler
but I don't give a fuck who he screws in private
I just wanna know who he's screwin in public
robbin, stealin, cheatin,
white collar criminal McDonald eatin
saxophone playin Yes Men sayin
"Boss you can really play horn well"
Hell no!

never

For just about anything they can bust us
false advertising sayin halls of justice
you get four years if you're Michael Milken
but ten to fifteen if you rob the milkman
take the children livin among us
teach em the truth about Christopher Columbus
take the army trained for warfare
build an army that's trained for healthcare
always evolutionary
sometimes revolutionary
always nonpollutionary definitely hallucinary
"But we keep movin on"

false advertising sayin halls of justice

Say Mary, Mary quite contrary
Mary, Mary quite contrary
are ya gonna sing for me now "yeah!"
are ya gonna sing for me now "yeah!"
    Don't know why there is no sun up in the sky
    Stormy weather! Yee Haaah!

but don't mistake our anger for resentment
don't mistake bein docile for contentment
don't mistake the bass for the treble tone
don't mistake Ross Perot on the speaker phone
don't mistake it when you hear us bein quiet
don't mistake uprising for a race riot
don't mistake a mirage for what you're shootin at
I often mistake Republicans and Democrats

try to talk it out, try to right it out

don't mistake the bass for the treble tone

forward ever backward never
this is what we say when we hit the stormy weather

Michael Franti

Slot Machine

CASH

Quarters

Gonna do the laundry
he says

he says
Gets on the highway
lighted like a landing strip
lighted like a landing strip
the slate of darkness scribbled on with a neon pen
somebody's cartoon car
flyin thru analog Ann Landers land
flyin thru infrastructure
flyin thru statistical abstracts of the
United States past encryption past the
bank machine past past lives into the
beating heart of the last days of the
twentieth century he comes to a
slot machine
CASH

CASH

CASH CASH

Who knows where his heart is
His heart was ripped out and
buried in a mattress stuffed with cash
he guesses
he guesses/every couple of weeks he
takes the metal detector out to
the national park
hikes up to the big chasm that separates
us and them
which the founding mothers and fathers
did not envision
which nobody thought would happen
wonder how it happened
wonder how it happened

how'd the rich get that rich
how'd the poor get that poor
how did everybody get so murderous
how'd everybody get so ready to kill
over the stupidest shit
he thinks it must come down to CASH

must be everything comes down to CASH

in this country anyway
in this country anyway
to avoid misery

Pulls into the parking lot
lots of money in his pocket
gets a drink
drinks it
drinks it
drinks it
and the quarters
go in
the slot
machine
and the quarters
gets a drink
drinks it
drinks it
drinks it
and the quarters
go in

CASH

Quarters, quarters

he says
Takin the car
he says

lighted like a landing strip
lighted like a landing strip

somebody's cartoon car
flyin thru dark dark digital backyards
flyin thru bank's glass door
flyin thru bankrupt economies
emptified ghetto streets made morbid by
gut reaction of kids backed by gat not by gold
not by God

slot machine. CASH
cash machine
CASH

CASH

CASH

His heart is in a bus station locker
His heart his remains he says he says
he questions he questions things but no
answers ever seem to come he knows
religion is not the solution
every couple of minutes
postal worker massacre
slaughtering law firms court rooms
where does it end
how does it happen

wonder how it happened
wonder how it happened

how'd the rich get that rich
how'd the poor get that poor
how did everybody get so murderous
how'd everybody get so ready to kill
over the stupidest things

he thinks it must come down to CASH

must be everything comes down to CASH
CASH CASH
everything comes down to this:

CASH

gets a drink
drinks it
drinks it
drinks it
and the quarters
go in
the slot
machine
gets a drink
drinks it
drinks it
drinks it
and the quarters
go in

the slot
machine　　　　　　75

CASH

                    orange cherry lemon
                    orange cherry lemon　　80
                    cherry lemon lemon
                    cherry lemon lemon
                    cherry lemon lemon
                    cherry lemon lemon

cherry cherry blank　　　　　　orange cherry blank
lemon orange lemon　　85　　　orange cherry blank
orange orange lemon　　　　　orange cherry orange
lemon lemon orange　　　　　　orange cherry lemon
lemon orange lemon　　　　　　orange cherry blank
lemon orange lemon　　　　　　orange cherry blank
orange cherry lemon　　90　　orange cherry cherry
orange orange lemon　　　　　orange cherry lemon
lemon lemon orange　　　　　　lemon blank cherry
blank blank cherry　　　　　　orange lemon blank
cherry cherry lemon　　　　　lemon blank cherry
blank blank cherry　　95　　orange lemon blank
blank cherry lemon　　　　　　cherry orange lemon
cherry blank lemon　　　　　　cherry orange lemon
cherry blank lemon　　　　　　cherry orange lemon
cherry blank cherry　　　　　cherry orange lemon
cherry blank blank　　100　　cherry orange lemon
cherry lemon lemon　　　　　　cherry orange lemon
cherry lemon lemon　　　　　　cherry orange lemon
orange lemon lemon　　　　　　cherry orange lemon
lemon cherry orange　　　　　cherry orange lemon
lemon cherry orange　　105　cherry orange lemon
lemon cherry orange　　　　　cherry orange lemon
lemon cherry orange　　　　　cherry orange lemon
lemon cherry orange　　　　　cherry orange lemon
lemon cherry orange　　　　　cherry orange lemon
cherry cherry cherry　　110　cherry cherry cherry

CASH　　　　　　　　　　　　　　CASH

he took the day off work
so he could be with his friends　115
Sammy and Davis　　　　　　　　Sammy and Davis
and ride around Telluride　　　and ride around Telluride
and ride around Vegas　　　　　and ride around Vegas
He says he wants to live　　　He says he wants to live
a life free of boredom　　120　a life free of boredom
a life free of pain　　　　　　a life free of pain
says this the U.S.
and there's money everywhere　and there's money everywhere

in the desert hills　　　125
in the darkest bar
in the deepest casket
in the poorest excuse
in the flat expression　　　　in the desert hills
in the fabrication　　　130　in the darkest bar
in the sliding land　　　　　in the deepest casket
in the Sands Hotel　　　　　　in the poorest excuse
I'm goin the store/　　　　　I'm goin the store/he says
takin the car　　　　　　　　takin the car
ignoring the index of　　135
economic indicators
and the statistics　　　　　and the statistics
that tell me I'm poor　　　that tell me I'm poor
I'm goin the store　　　　　I'm goin the store
I'm goin the store　　140　I'm goin the store
I'm goin the store　　　　　I'm goin the store
　　　　　　　　　　　　　　　isn't that what money's for?

Emily XYZ

149

Besmilr Brigham

Tell Our Daughters

each is beautiful
a woman's life
makes it (that awareness)
through her touch

        descendants
of strict age
set against vanity

not secure in loveliness

a girl is born
like a little bird opening its wing
she lifts her face
in a down of feathers

a rose
        opens its leaves
with such a natural care
that we give words for
petal deep
in the imagination
                a word becomes
                a bitter thing
                or a word is
                an imagination

tell our daughters   they are
fragile as a bird
strong as the rose
deep as a word

and let them make
their own growing time

                big with tenderness
the fire of love

The Good Shepherd

I lift the boy's body
from the trunk,
set it down,
then push it over the embankment
with my foot.
I watch it roll
down into the river
and feel I'm rolling with it,
feel the first cold slap of the water,
wheeze and fall down on one knee.
So tired, so cold.
Lord, I need a new coat,
not polyester, but wool,
new and pure
like the little lamb
I killed tonight.
With my right hand,
that same hand that hits
with such force,
I push myself up gently.
I know what I'd like—
some hot cocoa by the heater.

Once home, I stand at the kitchen sink,
letting the water run
till it overflows the pot,
then I remember the blood
in the bathroom
and so upstairs.
I take cleanser,
begin to scrub
the tub, tiles, the toilet bowl,
then the bathroom.
Mop, vacuum, and dust rag.
Work, work for the joy of it,
for the black boys
who know too much,
but not enough to stay away,
and sometimes a girl, the girls too.
How their hands
grab at my ankles, my knees.
And don't I lead them
like a good shepherd?
I stand at the sink,
where the water is still
overflowing the pot,
turn off the faucet,
then heat the water and sit down.
After the last sweet mouthful of chocolate
burns its way down my throat,
I open the library book,
the one on mythology,
and begin to read.
Saturn, it says, devours his children.
Yes, it's true, I know it.
An ordinary man, though, a man like me
eats and is full.
　　　Only God is never satisfied.

Ai

The Complete "United States of Poetry"
(American Sign Language Version)
in a Minute and a Half

Ahem

Translate every poem in the series into ASL?
and
I get a minute and a half to do it?
Better start by spelling it out for you Hearies
"WELCOME TO THE UNITED STATES OF POETRY!"

In a poem the words don't stand still
The "Y" of poetry
flies into meaning
collides with the ear of
the huddled masses yearning to hear
got a Brand New Dictionary
and a Flame of Truth to read it by.
But the poem takes flight outta sight
a winged "Y"

First stop: Down South
polin' down Word River
don't need to say it
let the band play it
watch the music

The poet makes a microphone
out of air
and just as the massive croon is ready to erupt
tiny "y" of poetry flies out

The poem is inside the music, see
and once set free
rides the wild ride
in perpetuity
rides it like a buckin' bronc
a jeep honk
in a honky tonk

let those cowboy poets
take us way out West
those are poem bullets
strapped to my vest
a shot it the air
Is a caption for {**!@#!##!!*&%!}
(Well, I swear)
Whadaya do when you hit Vegas
Let the slot machine windows spin
Spinnish to finish the poem
That's the jackpot!

Riding the wave of a poem all the way to the Pacific
Not even the ocean can stop us!
Surfing the streams of consciousness
My surfboard head in the dryer at the laundromat
Can this be Hollywood?
Poetry's "Y" finds a home in the HOLL WOOD sign
I was in Hollywood, where all the poems go
To be turned into box office smash hits
Poets sure get treated great out here
Make-up is the same as editing
The crowd roars and the cameras roll
As I smoosh a haiku into the cement:

New definition
For a concrete poem writ
Ten in flashbulb light

Hightail it out, fast as a trout,
The poem flies up the coast
The arc of Truth is the Bridge to Beauty
Get San Francisco to hold still long enough
To have a cuppa poetry
Where stimuli rise from the wisps
Weave a beret goatee
Explode into brainstorms
Drenching the City with poetry

The poem becomes the thing itself!
You know, writing could be allegorized as
Scaling the mountain of Pure Understanding

And the bird I see
Is the bird I be
Flying free
The trout below mimics my flight
I want to be
The diving point
Where Meaning claws into me
Clinging to understanding all you can say is

{WOW!}

Sight touches—is that sound I see?
Wild wolf howls transcend harmonies
Poem travels back in time
Indian appears—original rhyme
Vision snares a hurricane of antlers
The bow is the poem, the arrow is the poem
The elk is the poem
And their union creates the earth

And who is this,
Harvesting his crop of poetry
Can you dig it
The poet hisself
And my personal Muse,
Er, I mean "moo-se"
My cow
Blow these horns of Poetry, Mooster

Your "little letter Y" bird
Motors the ink link, and peanut butters
Face to life in the Capitol of US of Poetry,
Washington, DC, Lincoln's Memorial,
Note Abe's fingers sign his initials, "AL"
A deaf sculptor carved them there
Crash land on Lincoln's mole
Speechless poetry speaks with Lincoln's voice...
Whew! That was close!
Time to wave the wave.
Poetry flies into its shadow
The last image is the sound of poetry's shadow
As everything's shadow disappears back into your TV
May I direct you please
Back to your journey
Through "The United States of Poetry"

Peter Cook

155

Portraits

"Is that a real poem or did you just make it up your-self?"* is a question only poets can answer. "Who is a poet?" is another question, "What is a poem?" is the answer. You can't answer a question with a question is a truism, a philosophical conundrum, a rote response, and therefore not a poem. Ahem.

Poetry activist Luís J. Rodriguez, Jr., has said that "Everyone is a poet. The ability to write a poem is inborn, and anyone can do it." While you are writing a poem, you are a poet. Are you a poet when you put the quill down, when the Screensaver comes up on your laptop and you head for the refrigerator (book-shelf) for some inspiration?

Sometimes the answer is not related to the question. A physicist once told me that the greatest haiku of all time was $E=mc^2$. Is there a place where art meets science, dances the dance of the universes, the gyres of being and doing, of it and about it and tag you are it?

Certainly, in The United States of Poetry, poetry has met television and thus introduced new possibilities for both: a sense of relevance, for starters. But on our voyage through these states to film the show, it was meeting the poets, hearing them, seeing the ease with which they took the role of poet and lived in it like clothes, that inspired us.

The portraits that follow are not connected by theme, region, or aesthetic, but simply by the fact that they are of poets. These are real poems, and portraits of the poets who just made them up.

---

*These apocryphal words first appeared in print as the title of an essay by Robert Creeley, published as "Sparrow #40" by Black Sparrow Press in 1976.

THE POETS

JULI YANCY is twenty-two and lives in Omaha. This is her first published poem....KELL ROBERTSON has been a rodeo cowboy, a c & w singer, and is the first man on a horse to get killed off in Sam Peckinpah's *The Wild Bunch*. He has always been a poet. Currently somewhere on the road in the Southwest....MAUREEN OWEN lives in Guilford, Connecticut, and works for Inland Books, one of the foremost names in poetry distribution. She was coordinator of the St. Marks Poetry Project during the 1970s and is publisher of Telephone Books and Magazine....LINDA HASSELSTROM is a poet, an essayist, and a working ranch woman. Winner of the Western American Writer award, she lives in western South Dakota....KEITH WIL-SON is the Poet Laureate of Las Cruces, New Mexico. His credentials range from Beat to Cowboy to university prof. He has inspired many poets, including Denise Chávez and Kell Robertson....MIKE ROMOTH slacks in Seattle....WALLACE McRAE, the "Cowboy Curmudgeon," is the classic cow-boy poet and wrote what many consider the classic contemporary cowboy poem, "Reincarnation." He is the first cowboy poet to receive a National Heritage Award. Wally still works the family ranch in Forsyth, Montana.... MICHELE M. SERROS traveled with the Spoken Word Tent of Lollapalooza in 1994. She performs with the spoken word collective Guava Breasts in her native L.A....D-KNOWLEDGE (Derrick I. M. Gilbert) raps and rolls in L.A. He has appeared on TV, at the Apollo, and at poetry and rap clubs across the country....The Cook Boys are still sitting on tiny curbs outside 7-11's in Milwaukee. From this perch SEAN McNALLY can see the best minds of his generation just hanging around, framed by Tim Cook, left, and Matt Cook, right. They have traveled to National Slams and then forgotten to show up to read....MIKE TYLER was born and raised in New York City. The "most dangerous writer in America," he once broke his arm while reading (resulting in the poem "Logic Broke My Arm"). He was poetry director and editor of *American Idealism Rag* at the seminal downtown N.Y.C. poetry anti-salon, ABC No Rio....MARC SMITH is the creator of Slam. An ex-con-struction worker who lives in Chicago, he can still be found every Sunday running the show at the exquisite Green Mill Tavern....Poet/shaman/ activist/rocker JOHN TRUDELL has two best-selling CD's to his credit: *Graffiti Man* and *Johnny Damas & Me*. He is a founding member of the American Indian Movement (AIM)....

Untitled Nebraska Poem

Juli Yancy

Mama said that
during the depression they
were happy to put
lard on their bread as opposed to
butter and flour sack dresses didn't
itch if you used plenty of
vaseline.
And it was a greasy time breeding
greasy people and
in the fifties they were drunk all the time,
Mama said.
Everybody was.
And you did it with anyone
you pleased because
there was nothing to fill the
need, Mama said, in this
Nebraska.
In these fields.
So you married a black man,
liking to think that he was making you
cosmopolitan
with every stroke.
And you bore children out of confusion and
you still got drunk all the time,
Mama said. In
this Nebraska. In this
Nebraska.
In these fields.

THE OLD MAN GOES HOME

Under the discount store
the fast food place
the furniture outlet
under all that asphalt
is one of the best chunks
of black bottom farm land
in southeast Kansas.
My grandad grew corn
wheat, oats and alfalfa,
rotating the crops by
his almanac and the taste
of the dirt, and there
under that corner
my grandma's garden grew.
The house was somewhere
near the bicycle rack
and the barn was where
they have that bank
of video games.

Under all this asphalt and concrete
plastic and steel, I learned to cut
a calf, learned to drive a team of horses,
learned to work in this earth
and in that barn, learned
from a third cousin who
teetered on the edge of womanhood
another meaning for kisses
beyond the peck on the cheek
I got from grandma.

I close my eyes and see it,
butt my way under that old Jersey cow
squirt the hot steaming milk
into the cold tin bucket, hear
the hogs snorting around for slops
we saved for them.

I open my eyes and almost
get run over by a housewife
with a buggy full of disposable diapers
and sugar-coated cereals.

The security guard takes my arm, asks
if I'm alright, leads me out into the parking lot
asks me what I'm doing there if I'm not
going to buy anything.

I'm visiting my grandad's farm I say
underneath all this crap
is the sweetest little farm
in southeast Kansas.

Walking away
into the shimmering heat
rising from the parking lot
I swear I hear
grandma calling us for supper.
There'll be beans and cornbread
and iced tea...tomorrow we'll start
plowing the lower forty.
Then we'll come home and sit
on the front porch, watching the dogs
playing in the yard, dreaming
of going to town next week
to sell some hay and get
a store-bought hat
to wear at the dance at the Grange Hall.
Maybe my cousin will be there
and she'll teach me more
about this kissing business.

Right now
looking back at the parking lot
full of people doing something

all I can see is what we've lost.

Kell Robertson

POSTURE

When you're down and under and crushed and shattered
smashed and trodden and beaten, bamboozled, kicked and
destroyed   lost out, gone mad, fell back, shot up,
done in, wiped out   When your heart is broken   and
your nose is running, your days are numbered, your lot
is cast, you're wasted, worried, choked up and ruined
left out, disinherited, sweating, frustrated, alone and
demolished, hopeless, despairing, depressed and insane
you're lousy   you know it   you wish you could change
Your coat's ripped, your nose is crooked, your brain is
mush, your hands are cursed, your life is worthless
and you're uncomfortable   a hunchback, a sucker,
a recluse, a frog   When you know you can't make it
You're hideous, helpless, pusillanimous, squirrelly and
dumb

just bear in mind
that 9/10s of everything
is posture

Stand up!

Maureen Owen

The Only Place

The only place a woman can go to be alone
is the bathroom.
A woman would like to be wrapped in strong arms
when she cries, without having to explain,
or huddle on the couch wrapped in a blanket and a cat.
But all over America, women crouch instead
on a white, cold monument to wasting water.
We lean against a chilled tile wall,
stare at ourselves in an icy mirror,
flush the toilet to cover howls and curses,
brush our teeth twice to cover the taste of anger.
We lock the door, fill the tub with hot bubbles,
take a long time shaving our legs and armpits,
study the way waves break over bulging stomachs.
We scour the sink and rearrange the bottles under it,
refold towels, throw away old prescriptions,
count bandaids and bottles of suntan lotion.
We turn out the lights, stare into candle flames,
light incense, try to pretend we've taken our troubles
to a glowing temple, placed them in the lap
of a smiling golden Goddess.

Outside, men—who wouldn't know what to do
if a woman curled up in bed and cried—
can relax before bloodless images on TV
and think, "She's only in the bathroom
doing some woman's thing."
Behind a locked door, a woman
spins the empty toilet paper roll
like a Tibetan prayer wheel,
chanting "Help me, help me, help me."

Linda Hasselstrom

Desert Cenote

There is sadness among the stones
today, the rabbits are silent.

No wind. The heat bears down.
It has not rained for one year.

We have faith out here, desert
people, we wait, knowing with sureness

the swift cross of clouds, the blessings
of moisture (to deprive a man is to give

charms to him). I love this dry land
am caught even by blowing sand, reaches

of hot winds. I am not the desert
but its real name is not so far from mine.

Keith Wilson

The Patience Sutra

Come on
Let's steal a car
   and drive to the mountains
Let's do it   right now
We'll buy a bottle of wine
   and sit on a railroad bridge
      and sing songs to the moon
We'll find a fuse
   and we'll set it on fire
Come on   right now
     Let's go
       Let's go
Coffee cigarettes whiskey sex
Let's eat everything that makes us crazy
Come on   we've got to go
We can't wait even a minute more
Tonight is the end of the world
So let's dodge this catatonia
     that sings us into dangerous sleep

We can sleep when we're dead
We can diet
    when famine rolls into town
Enough of this comfort and anesthesia
Enough of insurance
   car payments
     love money
      deadlines
Can't you see the beautiful body
   you've been assigned
Don't you want to test it?
   Run it like a race car?
Let's go
   Let's go
     Right now
I don't want to read a book
   see a movie
     watch TV
Let's get in a fistfight
   you and I
Let's go down to the ocean
   it's not that far away
We'll strip off our clothes there
   and swim in the icy bitter sea
And if we cut our feet on the rocks
   so be it
And if we lose ourselves in the waves
   so be it
But let's do it now
   Let's go
     Let's go
Who here is afraid to explode?
Let's buy a gun
Let's break a window
Let's take our bicycles
   to the top of the hill
     and ride down—no hands
    cruising through the red lights
    with our eyes closed
We could all get tattoos
   I know a place nearby
We could all be on the next ferry
   to Alaska
Let's do it all
Come on
   Let's go

Mike Romoth

The Coyote

If you get back off the interstates
And away from urban trends,
You'll find a coyote doesn't have
A multitude of friends.

But I kind of like to see one,
Or hear him greet the day.
He's sort of part of our old West
That's fading fast away.

Though he demands his tribute
I'll let him have his due.
Let him take his cut, and welcome.
I guess it's his world, too.

Wallace McRae

Tag Banger's Last Can

Flaco held his manhood
steady.
Aimed it at
a city block
pissing boosted Krylon
citrus yellow
cherry red
black.

His defiant stand
earned him
a loyal crew
customized baseball cap
t.v. tabloid exposé
and a toe tag.

Michele M. Serros

The Revolution Will Be on the Big Screen

My man Gil Scott-Heron once said:
The revolution will not be televised
Well...
Gil Scott may have a point
The revolution may not be televised
But...
The revolution will be a major motion picture
The revolution will not be televised
But...
The revolution will be on the big screen

The Revolution will be a fifty million dollar production
The Revolution will be written by John Grisham
And directed by Oliver Stone
The Revolution will star Kevin Costner and Julia Roberts
And they will teach people of color
How to revolt
And how to fight and how to hide and how to kill
And how to SCREAM
The Revolution will be on the big screen, brother.

The Revolution will have one Latino extra
Playin' a thief
One Asian extra
Playin' a servant
And one Native American extra runnin'
down Florence and Normandie yellin'
Geronimo.

The Revolution will have one Black supporting actor
Denzel Washington
Who will be killed by Kevin Costner in the first
three minutes
For looking at Julia Roberts for more than
one minute
While Kevin Costner will have a picture of Whitney Houston
Burnin' in his wallet
The Revolution will be on the big screen, sistah.

D-Knowledge
(Derrick I. M. Gilbert)

The Revolution will be coming soon to a theatre near you
And will get two thumbs up from Siskel and Ebert
And will make more money than Jurassic Park and ET
The Revolution will cost $7.50 to see or $5.50 if
you got a student i.d.
The Revolution will go good with popcorn, bon bons and licorice
The Revolution will be on the big screen.

The Revolution will have a multi-platinum soundtrack
Wtih revolutionary songs sung by
Guns 'N' Roses, Metallica and Madonna
The Revolution will be advertised on billboards, buses, t-shirts
and at Taco Bell and Micky Dees
The Revolution will be on the big screen.

The Revolution will be distributed internationally
The Revolution will be seen in Cuba, Rwanda and Haiti
The Revolution will change the way the world thinks about
Revolution
And the way the world thinks about
Change
The Revolution will be on the big screen.

The Revolution will have a sequel
The Revolution will have a part III
The Revolution will be too large for t.v.
Too large for the little screen
The Revolution will be larger than life
Larger than large
And larger than larger than large
The Revolution will not be televised
Will not be televised
Not be televised
Be televised
The Revolution will be
On the Big Screen.

THE BEST MINDS OF OUR GENERATION

I've seen the best minds of our generation and they're loitering outside. That guy over there in the white tube socks with the pubic hair mustache? He does brilliant work. The fella next to him in the Adidas shirt with the beer gut, he's got a good head on his shoulders, he really does, you know he does, just look at him. And that man with the black cowboy hat in the tight jeans, he's got a fresh outlook, a whole new perspective. Yep, there go the best minds of our generation, just poking around in the street.

Sean McNally

Trial by Ice

The not-breathing
are not the only ones
not breathing
I know this is obvious
so is not walking under a falling anvil
(what is an anvil?)
if you saw someone about to walk
under a falling anvil
would you say
"hey, don't walk under a falling anvil"
or would you not want to say it
cause you didn't want to be obvious
cliches are skunk farts
bum
bard of the "of course" curse
ed
by the too far-in garage
the sins of the apparent
bored into the chilly
if I'm not not
repeating myself
I don't think I've used
the obvious badly
smoke from a fire
does cause me
to think "fire"
is it o.k.
to yell "fire"
is it o.k.
to yell "fire"
at a fire
"Fire!"

Mike Tyler

Underdog

Marc Smith

I'm for the little guy—
Blue black tan gray green red white.
I'm for the guy that lost the fight
That day on the school yard
When the bully stole the nerd's hat,
And the nerd let him have it—
The hat that is. And it wasn't right.
Demanded fight.
So the little guy Nobody stepped forward
And said, "Hey, you can't do things like that."
And the bully laughed, "Oh yeah. Watch this!"
And pushed Nobody's face/into the chain link fence;
Massaged it there/while the nerd looked on
Mewling,/"It's only a hat. It's only a hat."
Until the little guy Nobody
Had had enough of being a hero,
Feeling the knots of the chain link fence
Cut into his cheek,
And called it quits.

I'm for that guy
Walkin' away feelin' like shit.
Feelin' as if he'd lost somethin'
Losin' to a guy twice his size—
Because, in the movies
A real hero chops those bullies down,
Sets right the situation.

But it never worked out that way for this kid
Righteous though he was.
And in his lifetime he found out
That the bullies were always winning.
And the nerds were always helpless.
And caught between them,
Forever pathetically engaged,
Were guys like him
Trying to set things right,
Trying to undo the damage,
Trying to live in accordance with ancient ideals
That even in ancient times
Must have been just that,
Ideals.

But what the hell. I'm for him,
Whoever he is—
Because, even today,
When it comes to a stolen hat,
A stolen chance,
A stolen you name it,
He stands up right in the face of it,
Come what may, and says,
"Hey. Hey. You can't do things like that!"

INVOCATION

We are from the Halluca Nation
We are the tribe that they can not see
We live on an industrial reservation

We are the Halluca Nation
We have been called the Indian
We have been called Native American

We have been called Hostile
We have been called Pagan
We have been called Militant
We have been called everything but who we are

We are the Halluca Nation
The human beings
They can not see us, but we can see them

We are the Halluca Nation
Our D.N.A. is of earth and sky
Our D.N.A. is of the past and the future

We are the Halluca Nation
We are the evolution
The continuation

We are the Halluca Nation

John Trudell

Index of Poets

Ai: *Blackout* (W. W. Norton, 1995); *Greed* (W. W. Norton, 1993); *Fate* (Houghton Mifflin Co., 1991); *Sin* (Houghton Mifflin Co., 1986); *Cruelty* (Houghton Mifflin Co., 1979); *Killing Floor* (Houghton Mifflin Co., 1979)

Luís Alfaro: performances, *Theatre Offensive* (Boston, 1993); *Bitter Homes and Gardens* (New Theatre Works Festival, 1992); *Deep in the Crotch of My Latino Psyche* (Highways Performance Space, 1992); *Josie's Cabaret* (San Francisco, 1992); *Straight as a Line* (Mentor Reading, 1992)

Miguel Algarín: *Time's Now/Ya Es Tiempo* (Akira Nogami, 1992); *Body Bee Calling* (Arte Publico Press, 1982); *On Call* (Arte Publico Press, 1980); *Mongo Affair* (Nuyorican Poets Café Press, 1978); Pablo Neruda, *Song of Protest,* trans. Algarín (Quill, 1976)

Indran Amirthanayagam: *The Elephants of Reckoning* (Hanging Loose Press, 1993)

Amiri Baraka: *The Autobiography of LeRoi Jones* (Freundlich, 1984); *Black Magic* (Bobbs-Merrill, 1969); *Dutchman and the Slave* (William Morrow and Co. Inc., 1964); *Blues People* (William Morrow and Co. Inc., 1963); *Preface to a Twenty Volume Suicide Note* (Totem/Corinth, 1961)

Paul Beatty: *Joker Joker Deuce* (Penguin Books, 1994); *Big Bank Take Little Bank* (Nuyorican Poets Café Press, 1991)

Besmilr Brigham: *Heaved from the Earth* (New Directions Books, 1971)

Joseph Brodsky: *Watermark* (Farrar, Straus and Giroux, Inc., 1993); *To Urania* (Farrar, Straus and Giroux, Inc., 1988); *Less Than One* (Farrar, Straus and Giroux, Inc., 1986); *A Part of Speech* (Farrar, Straus and Giroux, Inc., 1977); *Selected Poems,* trans. George L. Kline (Harper and Row, 1973)

Jimmy Carter: *Always a Reckoning* (Times Books, 1995); *Talking Peace: A Vision for the Next Generation* (Penguin, 1993); *Turning Point: A Candidate, a State, and a Nation Come of Age* (Times Books, 1992); *The Blood of Abraham* (University of Arkansas, 1985); *Keeping Faith: Memoirs of a President* (Bantam Doubleday Dell, 1982)

Sandra Cisneros: *Loose Woman* (Vintage, 1995); *La Casa en Mango Street* (Vintage, 1994); *My Wicked Wicked Ways* (Turtle Bay, 1992; Third Woman, 1987); *Woman Hollering Creek and Other Stories* (Vintage, 1992); *The House on Mango Street* (Vintage, 1991); *Bad Boys* (Mango Press, 1980)

Pearl Cleage: *Deals with the Devil and Other Reasons to Riot* (Ballantine Books, 1992); *Mad at Miles: A Black Woman's Guide to Truth* (The Cleage Group, 1990); *The Brass Bed and Other Stories* (Third World Press, 1990); *Live at Club Zebra: The Book,* vol. 1 (Just Us Theatre, 1988)

Michélle T. Clinton: *Black Sage: The Womb and the Water* (Pennywhistle Press, 1995); *Good Sense and the Faithless* (West End Press, 1994); *High Blood/Pressure* (West End Press, 1986)

Leonard Cohen: *Stranger Music: Selected Poems and Songs* (McClelland and Stewart Inc., 1993); *Book of Mercy* (McClelland and Stewart Inc., 1984); *The Favourite Game* (New Canadian Library, 1973); *Beautiful Losers* (Viking, 1966); *The Spice Box of Earth* (McClelland and Stewart Inc., 1961)

Wanda Coleman: *American Sonnets* (Light and Dust Press, 1994); *Hand Dance* (Black Sparrow Press, 1993); *African Sleeping Sickness: Stories and Poems* (Black Sparrow Press, 1990); *A War of Eyes and Other Stories* (Black Sparrow Press, 1988); *Heavy Daughter Blues* (Black Sparrow Press, 1986)

Peter Cook: performances, *Your Eyes My Hands* (Chicago, 1994); with Kenny Lerner, *Flying Words*

Dennis Cooper: *The Dream Police: 1969–1983* (Grove Press, 1995); *Wrong* (Grove Press, 1993); *Frisk* (Grove Press, 1991); *Try* (Grove Press, 1991); *Idols* (Amethyst Press, Inc., 1989; The Sea Horse Press, 1979)

Robert Creeley: *Life and Death* (Gagosian Gallery, 1993*); The Selected Poems of Robert Creeley* (University of California Press, 1991); *The Collected Poems of Robert Creeley 1945–1975* (University of California Press, 1982); *Pieces* (Charles Scribner's Sons, 1969); *For Love: Poems, 1950–1960* (Charles Scribner's Sons, 1962)

Nora Marks Dauenhauer: *The Droning Shaman* (The Black Current Press, 1988)

Johnny Depp: films, *Ed Wood* (Disney, 1994); *Benny and Joon* (Metro Goldwyn Mayer, 1993); *What's Eating Gilbert Grape* (Paramount, 1993); *Edward Scissorhands* (20th Century Fox, 1990); *A Nightmare on Elm Street* (New Line Cinema, 1984)

Nerissa Diaz: in *Word Up,* ed. Zoe Anglesey (El Centro de la Raza, 1992)

Rita Dove: *Mother Love* (W. W. Norton, 1995); *The Darker Face of the Earth* (Story Line Press, 1994); *Selected Poems* (Pantheon/Vintage, 1993); *Grace Notes* (W. W. Norton, 1989); *Thomas and Beulah* (Carnegie-Mellon University Press, 1986)

Larry Eigner: *Windows/Walls/Yard/Ways* (Black Sparrow Press, 1994); *Water, Places, a Time* (Black Sparrow Press, 1983); *The World and Its Streets, Places* (Black Sparrow Press, 1977); *Anything on Its Side* (The Elizabeth Press, 1974); *Things Stirring Together or Far Away* (Black Sparrow Press, 1974)

Maggie Estep: *Diary of a Lunachick* (Harmony Books, 1995); recordings, *No More Mr. Nice Girl* (Nuyo/Imago, 1994)

Lawrence Ferlinghetti: *These Are My Rivers: New and Selected Poems, 1955–1993* (New Directions Books, 1993); *European Poems and Transitions* (New Directions Books, 1988); *Back Roads to Far Places* (New Directions Books, 1971); *A Coney Island of the Mind* (New Directions Books, 1958); *Pictures of the Gone World* (City Lights, 1955)

Ruth Forman: *We Are the Young Magicians* (Beacon Press, 1993)

Michael Franti: recordings, Spearhead, *Home* (Capitol Records, 1994*);* Disposable Heroes of Hiphoprisy, *Hipocracy Is the Greatest Luxury* (Island Records, 1992); Beatnigs, *Beatnigs* (Island Records, 1988)

Allen Ginsberg: *Cosmopolitan Greetings: Poems 1986–1993* (Harper-Collins, 1994); *Howl Annotated* (Harper and Row, 1986); *White Shroud Poems 1980–1985* (Harper and Row, 1986); *Collected Poems 1947–1980* (HarperCollins, 1984); *Howl and Other Poems* (City Lights, 1956)

John S. Hall: recordings, King Missile, *King Missile* (Atlantic, 1994); King Missile, *Happy Hour* (Atlantic, 1992); King Missile, *The Way to Salvation* (Atlantic, 1991); King Missile, *Mystical Shit* (Shimmy Disc, 1990); King Missile, *Dog Fly Religion* (Shimmy Disc, 1988)

Carla Harryman: *There Never Was a Rose Without a Thorn* (City Lights, 1995); *Memory Play* (O Books, 1994); *In the Mode Of* (Zasterle Press, 1991); *Animal Instincts* (This Press, 1989); *Property* (Tuumba Press, 1979)

Linda Hasselstrom: *Dakota Bones: Collected Poems* (Spoon River Poetry Press, 1993); *Land Circle: Writings Collected from the Land* (Fulcrum, Inc., 1991); *Roadkill* (Spoon River Poetry Press, 1987)

Jack Kerouac: *The Scripture of the Golden Eternity* (City Lights, 1994); *Poems All Sizes* (City Lights, 1992); *Mexico City Blues* (Grove Press, 1990); *Scattered Poems* (City Lights, 1970)

Russell Leong: *Desiring Asian Americans: Dimensions of the Gay and Lesbian Experience,* ed. Russell Leong (Routledge, 1995); *The Country of Dreams and Dust* (West End Press, 1993); *Moving the Image: Independent Asian Pacific American Media Arts 1970–1990,* ed. Russell Leong (UCLA and Visual Communications, 1991)

Genny Lim: *Island: Poetry and History of Chinese Immigrants on Angel Island, 1910–1940,* ed. Genny Lim (University of Washington, 1991); *Winter Place* (Kearny Street Press, 1989)

Selected Bibliography

George Ella Lyon: *Here and Then* (Orchard, 1994); *Mama Is a Miner* (Orchard, 1994); *Catalpa* (Wind Publications, 1993); *Who Came Down That Road?* (Orchard, 1992); *Mountain* (Andrew Mountain Press, 1983)

Lypsinka (John Epperson): performances, *Ballet of the Dolls*; *Dial 'M' for Model*

Wallace McRae: *Cowboy Curmudgeon* (Gibbs Smith, 1992); *Up North Is Down the Creek* (Museum of the Rockies, 1985); *It's Just Grass and Water* (Shawn Higgins, 1979)

Czeslaw Milosz: *A Year of the Hunter* (Farrar, Straus and Giroux, Inc., 1994); *Provinces* (The Ecco Press, 1991); *The Collected Poems: 1931–1987* (The Ecco Press, 1988); *Unattainable Earth* (The Ecco Press, 1985); *Bells in Winter* (The Ecco Press, 1978)

Tracie Morris: *Chap-T-Her Won* (TM Ink, 1993)

Thylias Moss: *Somewhere Else Right Now* (Dial Books for Young Readers, 1995); *Small Congregations: New and Selected Poems* (The Ecco Press, 1993); *I Want To Be* (Dial Books for Young Readers, 1993); *Rainbow Remnants in Rock Bottom Ghetto Sky* (Persea, 1991)

Sheryl Noethe: with Jack Collom, *Poetry Everywhere* (Teachers and Writers Collaborative, 1994); *The Descent of Heaven Over the Lake* (New Rivers Press, 1984)

Jim Northrup: *Returning the Gift* (The University of Arizona Press, 1994); *Walking the Rez Road* (Voyageur Press, Inc., 1993)

Naomi Shihab Nye: *Benito's Dream Bottle* (Simon and Schuster Books for Young Readers, 1995); *Red Suitcase* (BOA Editions, 1994); *Sitti's Secrets* (Simon and Schuster, 1994) *Yellow Glove* (Breitenbush Books, 1986); *Hugging the Juke Box* (E. P. Dutton, 1982)

Maureen Owen: *Untapped Maps* (Potes and Poets Press, 1993); *Imaginary Income* (Hanging Loose Press, 1992); *Amelia Earhart* (Vortex Editions, 1987); *Zombie Notes* (Sun Press, 1986)

Willie Perdomo: *Where a Nickel Costs a Dime* (W. W. Norton, 1995)

Rev. Pedro Pietri: *Scarafaggi metropolitani e altre poesie* (Baldini and Castoldi, 1993); *The Masses Are Asses* (Waterfront Press, 1983); *Traffic Violations* (Waterfront Press, 1983); *Puerto Rican Obituary* (Monthly Review Press, 1973) *Invisible Poetry* (Downtown Train Publications, Written While on an Uptown Train, 1898).

Javier Piña: in *Word Up*, ed. Zoe Anglesey (El Centro de la Raza, 1992)

Dan Powers: *Good Earth and Poor* (October Release, 1995); *Christine Diablo's Eyes* (Penny Dreadful Press, 1994)

Vess Quinlan: *The Trouble with Dreams* (Wind Vein Press, 1992); *The Rosamond Papers* (Northeastern Oklahoma University Press, 1991)

Henry Real Bird: *Where Shadows Are Born* (University of Findlay, 1992)

Lou Reed: *Between Thought and Expression* (Hyperion Books, 1991); recordings, *Magic and Loss* (Sire Records/Warner Brothers Records, 1992) *Songs for 'Drella* (Sire Records, 1990); *New York* (Sire Records, 1989); *The Velvet Underground* (MGM, 1969); *White Light/White Heat* (Verve, 1967)

Kell Robertson: *Trailer Tramps* (Road House, 1992); with Ann Menebroker, *Mailbox Boogie* (Zerx Press, 1991); *Bear Crossing* (Guerilla Poetics, 1989); *Outlaw Fires* (Black Rabbit, 1989); *The Eyes of Jesse James* (Borracho Press, 1973)

Mike Romoth: *Tonsure* (Seattle Art Access, 1994)

Michele M. Serros: *Chicana Falsa* (Lalo Press, 1993)

Hal Sirowitz: *The Morning After* (Butthead Publications, 1994); *Fishnet Stockings* (Appearances, 1993); *No More Birthdays* (Bacchae Press, 1993); *Bedroom Wall* (Vendetta Press, 1992); *Girlie Pictures* (Low Tech Press, 1982)

Sparrow: *Test Drive* (Appearances, 1995); *My Cockroach Diary* (The Funny Times, 1994)

Peter Spiro: *The Story of Creation Told by Saint Louis the "Show Me" Saint* (1991); *Dancing with Grace* (X Press, 1990); *3 Guys* (1990); *Work* (1990)

James Still: *The Wolfpen Notebooks: A Record of Appalachian Life* (University Press of Kentucky, 1991); *The Wolfpen Poems* (Berea College Press, 1986); *River of Earth* (King Library Press, 1983; Viking, 1940); *The Man in the Bushes: The Notebooks of James Still, 1935–1987* (University Press of Kentucky); *Hounds on the Mountain* (Viking, 1937)

Everton Sylvester: recordings, Brooklyn Funk Essentials, *Cool and Steady and Easy* (RCA/BMG, 1995)

Jeff Tagami: *October Light* (Kearny Street Workshop Press, 1987)

Quincy Troupe: *Weather Reports* (Harlem River, 1991); with Miles Davis, *Miles* (Simon and Schuster, 1990); *James Baldwin: The Legacy*, ed. Quincy Troupe (Simon and Schuster, 1989); *Skulls Along the River* (I. Reed Books, 1984); *Snake-Back Solos* (I. Reed Books, 1978)

John Trudell: *Stickman* (Inanout Press, 1994); recordings, *Johnny Damas and Me* (Ryko, 1994); *AKA Graffiti Man* (Ryko, 1992)

Mike Tyler: *From Alabama to California* (The Art Cannot Be Damaged Press, 1993)

Derek Walcott: *The Fortunate Traveller* (Farrar, Straus and Giroux, Inc., 1990); *Omeros* (Farrar, Straus and Giroux, Inc., 1990); *Collected Poems: 1948–1984* (HarperCollins, 1986); *Midsummer* (Farrar, Straus and Giroux, Inc., 1984); *Selected Poems* (Farrar, Straus and Giroux, Inc., 1984)

Sue Wallis: *Another Green Grass Lover: Selected Poetry of Sue Wallis* (Dry Crik Press, 1994); *The Exalted One* (Dry Crik Press, 1991)

C. D. Wright: *Just Whistle* (Kelsey Street Press, 1993); *String Light* (University of Georgia Press, 1991); *Further Adventures with You* (Carnegie-Mellon University Press, 1986); *Translations of the Gospel Back into Tongues* (SUNY Press, 1982)

John Wright: *Brag from South Arapahoe Peak* (Boar Hog Press, 1993); *Bookstore Cowboys* (Snake Oil Press, 1991); *Red Meat* (Slough Press, 1989)

Emily XYZ: recordings, *Jimmy Page Loves Lori Maddox b/w Sinatra Walks Out* (Kill Rock Stars, 1995); *Who Shot Sadat* (Vinyl Repellant, 1982)

Lois-Ann Yamanaka: *Wild Meat and the Bully Burgers* (Farrar, Straus and Giroux, Inc., 1996); *Saturday Night at the Pahala Theatre* (Bamboo Ridge Press, 1994)

Photography Credits

Thomas Krueger, Principal Photography

Tami Reiker, Peter Agliata, Second Unit Photography; Chris Buck, Jeff Day, Paul Schoenberger, Location Photography; Ken Schles, Clock Photography

Text Credits

Ai: "The Good Shepherd: Atlanta, 1981," from *Sin.* Copyright © 1986 by Ai. Reprinted by permission of Houghton Mifflin Co. All rights reserved.

Miguel Algarín: From "HIV," in *ALOUD! Voices from the Nuyorican Poets Café,* ed. Miguel Algarín and Bob Holman (Henry Holt, 1994). Originally appeared in *Longshot* magazine.

Indran Amirthanayagam: From *The Open Boat: Poems from Asian America,* ed. David Mura (Anchor Books, 1993). Originally appeared in *Night Magazine.*

Amiri Baraka: From *The World* magazine.

Paul Beatty: From *Big Bank Take Little Bank* (Nuyorican Poets Café Press, 1991).

Joseph Brodsky: From *So Forth,* to be published by Farrar, Straus and Giroux, Inc. Poem copyright © 1989 by Joseph Brodsky. Reprinted by permission of Farrar, Straus and Giroux, Inc.

Elizabeth Barrett Browning: From "How Do I Love Thee?" in *Sonnets from the Portuguese.*

Lord Buckley: Reprinted by permission of Bizarre Records. Deep thanks to Oliver Trager for the transcript.

Jimmy Carter: From *Always a Reckoning* (Times Books, 1995).

Sandra Cisneros: By permission of Susan Bergholz Literary Services, New York. Courtesy *Bomb* magazine.

Michélle T. Clinton: From *Good Sense & the Faithless* (West End Press, 1994).

Leonard Cohen: Copyright © 1992 Leonard Cohen/Stranger Music, Inc. From Leonard Cohen, *The Future* (SONY, 1992) and *Stranger Music: Selected Poems and Songs* (McClelland and Stewart Inc., 1993).

Wanda Coleman: Copyright © 1993 by Wanda Coleman. Reprinted from *Hand Dance* by permission of Black Sparrow Press.

Peter Cook: Translated by Bob Holman and Liz Wolter.

Dennis Cooper: From *Idols* (The Sea Horse Press, 1979; Amethyst Press, 1989).

Robert Creeley: From *Life and Death* (Gagosian/The Grenfell Press, 1993).

e. e. cummings: From "but we've the may," in *Complete Poems: 1904-1962,* ed. George J. Firmage, by permission of Liveright Publishing Corporation. Copyright © 1963, 1991 by the Trustees for the E. E. Cummings Trust.

Richard Henry Dana: From "The Husband and the Wife's Grave," in *19th Century American Poetry,* ed. John Hollander (Voyager CD-ROM, 1994).

Nora Marks Dauenhauer: From *The Wicazo SA Review, A Journal of Indian Studies* (Cheney, Washington, 1989).

Nerissa Diaz: Courtesy El Centro de la Raza, Seattle.

Emily Dickinson: Reprinted by permission of the publishers from *The Letters of Emily Dickinson,* ed. Thomas H. Johnson, Cambridge, Massachusetts, The Belknap Press of Harvard University Press. Copyright © 1958, 1986 by the President and Fellows of Harvard College.

H. D. (Hilda Doolittle): From "At Baia." Copyright © 1957 by Norman Holmes Pearson. Reprinted by permission of New Directions Publishing Corporation.

Rita Dove: Reprinted from *Grace Notes* with the permission of the author and W. W. Norton and Company, Inc. Copyright © 1989 by Rita Dove.

Ralph Waldo Emerson: From journal, June 24-28, 1840, in *Emerson in His Journals,* ed. Joel Porte (Harvard University Press, 1984). Reprinted with permission. Thanks to Luís Rodriguez and Douglas Crase.

Maggie Estep: *Diary of a Lunachick* (Harmony Books, 1995).

Lawrence Ferlinghetti: From "I Am Waiting," in *These are My Rivers: New and Selected Poems, 1955-1993* (New Directions, 1993).

Ruth Forman: From *We Are the Young Musicians.* Copyright © 1993 by Ruth Forman. Reprinted by permission of Beacon Press.

Allen Ginsberg: From Allen Ginsberg, *Cosmopolitan Greetings: Poems 1986-1993* (HarperCollins, 1994).

Carla Harryman: From "Fish Speech," in *Memory Play* (O Books, 1994). Originally appeared in *Avec.*

Linda Hasselstrom: From *Land Circle: Writings Collected from the Land,* copyright © 1991. Fulcrum Publishing, Inc., Golden, Colorado.

Robinson Jeffers: From "Ave Caesar," in *The Selected Poetry of Robinson Jeffers* (Random House, 1972). Copyright © 1928, renewed 1959 by Robinson Jeffers. Reprinted by permission of the Estate of Robinson Jeffers.

Jack Kerouac: From *Mexico City Blues* (Grove Press, 1987)

Russell Leong: Originally appeared in *Positions: East Asia Cultures Critique,* ed. Tani Barlow (Duke University Press, spring 1993) and, in final form, in *The Country of Dreams and Dust* (West End Press, 1993).

Genny Lim: From *Winter Place* (Kearny Street Workshop, 1989).

Henry Wadsworth Longfellow: From "Paul Revere's Ride."

George Ella Lyon: From *Iron Mountain Review.*

Wallace McRae: From *Cowboy Curmudgeon* (Gibbs Smith, 1992).

Edna St. Vincent Millay: "First Fig," in *Collected Poems* (HarperCollins). Copyright © 1922, 1950 by Edna St. Vincent Millay. Used by permission of Elizabeth Barrett, literary executor.

Czeslaw Milosz: From *The Collected Poems: 1931-1987.* Copyright © 1988 by Czeslaw Milosz Royalties Inc. First printed by The Ecco Press in 1988. Reprinted with permission.

Marianne Moore: From *The Fables of La Fontaine,* translated by Marianne Moore. Copyright © Marianne Moore, 1952, 1953, 1954; copyright renewed by Marianne Moore, 1964; copyright renewed 1982 by Lawrence E. Brinn and Louise Crane, Executors of the Estate of Marianne Moore. Used by arrangement with Viking Penguin, a division of Penguin Books USA, Inc. And from *The Complete Works of Marianne Moore.* Used by permission of Faber and Faber Ltd.

Tracie Morris: From Tracie Morris, *Chap-T-Her Won* (TM Ink, 1993) and *ALOUD! Voices from the Nuyorican Poets Café,* ed. Miguel Algarín and Bob Holman (Henry Holt, 1994).

Thylias Moss: From Thylias Moss, *Rainbow Remnants in Rock Bottom Ghetto Sky.* Reprinted by permission of Persea Books.

Sheryl Noethe: Originally appeared in *Cutbank* magazine.

Jim Northrup: From *Walking the Rez Road* (Voyageur Press, Inc., 1993).

Frank O'Hara: From *Collected Poems of Frank O'Hara* (Alfred A. Knopf, 1971) and *Meditations in an Emergency,* reprinted by permission of Grove Press. Thanks to Maureen Granville-Smith, Administratrix of the Estate of Frank O'Hara.

Maureen Owen: Originally appeared in *Big Deal #5* magazine.

Dorothy Parker: "Theory," from *The Portable Dorothy Parker,* copyright © 1928, copyright renewed 1956 by Dorothy Parker. Used by permission of Viking Penguin, a division of Penguin Books USA Inc, and courtesy the NAACP.

Javier Piña: Courtesy El Centro de la Raza, Seattle.

Ezra Pound: From "Homage to Sextus Propertius." Copyright © 1926 by Ezra Pound; copyright © 1990 by Lea Baechler and A. Walton Litz. Reprinted by permission of New Directions Publishing Corporation.

Dan Powers: From *Kameleon* magazine.

Vess Quinlan: From *The Trouble with Dreams* (Wind Vein Press, 1992).

Henry Real Bird: From *Maverick Western Verse* (Gibbs Smith Books, 1994). Originally appeared in *Where Shadows Are Born* (University of Findlay, 1992).

Lou Reed: From *Between Thought and Expression* (Hyperion Books, 1991) and Lou Reed, *New York* (Sire Records, 1989).

Kenneth Rexroth: From "Time Is the Mercy of Eternity." Copyright © 1956 by New Directions Publishing Corporation.

Kell Robertson: From *Maverick Western Verse,* ed. John Doffelmeyer (Gibbs Smith Books, 1994). Originally appeared in *Dry Crick Review.*

Mike Romoth: From *Tonsure* (Seattle Art Access).

Hal Sirowitz: Originally appeared in *Zenos* magazine (England).

Sparrow: Originally appeared in *Sun* magazine.

Peter Spiro: From *Labor in the Post Industrial Age,* ed. Jim Villani and Naton Leslie (Pig Iron Press, 1990) and *ALOUD! Voices from the Nuyorican Poets Café,* ed. Miguel Algarín and Bob Holman (Henry Holt, 1994).

James Still: Copyright © 1986 by James Still. Reprinted from James Still, *The Wolfpen Poems,* by permission of Berea College Press. Originally appeared in James Still, *Hounds on the Mountain* (Viking Press, 1937).

Everton Sylvester: From Brooklyn Funk Essentials, *Cool and Steady and Easy* (RCA/BMG, 1995).

Jeff Tagami: From Jeff Tagami, *October Light* (Kearny Street Workshop Press, 1987) and *The Open Boat,* ed. David Mura (Anchor/Doubleday, 1993).

Sara Teasdale: From "What Do I Care 'Moonlight,'" in *The Collected Poems of Sara Teasdale* (Simon and Schuster, 1966). Reprinted by permission of Wellesley College.

Quincy Troupe: From Quincy Troupe, *Weather Reports: New and Selected Poems* (Harlem River Press, 1991).

John Trudell: From "Rockin the Rez," on John Trudell, *AKA Graffiti Man* (Ryko, 1992).

Derek Walcott: From *Collected Poems 1948-1984.* Copyright © 1986 by Derek Walcott. Reprinted by permission of Farrar, Straus and Giroux, Inc., and Faber and Faber Ltd.

Sue Wallis: From *Another Green Grass Lover: Selected Poetry of Sue Wallis* (Dry Crik Press, 1994).

Walt Whitman: From "I Hear America Singing."

William Carlos Williams: From "Asphodel, That Greeny Flower." Copyright © 1982, 1986 by William Eric Williams and Paul H. Williams. Reprinted by permission of New Directions Publishing Company. "If it ain't a pleasure, it ain't a poem" from Collected Recordings of William Carlos Williams, ed. Richard Swigg. Copyright © 1951 by William Carlos Williams. Used by permission of New Directions Publishing Corporation. Included on *The Poet's Voice,* ed. Stratis Havirias (Harvard University Press, 1978).

C. D. Wright: From *Translation of the Gospel Back into Tongues.* Reprinted by permission of the State University of New York Press. Copyright © 1983. Originally appeared in *Terrorism* (Lost Roads Books, 1979).

Emily XYZ: From *ALOUD! Voices from the Nuyorican Poets Café,* ed. Miguel Algarín and Bob Holman (Henry Holt, 1994).

Lois-Ann Yamanaka: From *Saturday Night at the Pahala Theatre* (Bamboo Ridge Press, 1994). By permission of Susan Bergholz Literary Services, New York.

Many people consulted, contributed info, expertise, and energy, among them: Guy Mendes, Jessica Hagedorn, Gary Glazner, Cathy Bowman, Andy Biskin, Roberto Bedoya, Jason Shinder, Robert Polito, Lois Griffith, Josefina Ramirez, David Shapiro, Walter Lew, Joyce Nako, Ron Padgett, Bienvenida Matias, Angela Fontanez, Jackie Leopold, Marina Gonzalez, Nicky Tamrong, Susan Robeson, Arthur Sze, Anne Waldman, David Cope, D. H. Melhem, Michael Warr, Lisa Buscani, Julie Guilden, Bill Adler, Slim Moon, Xavier Cavazos, Hamish Todd, Rick Tejeta-Flores, Robert Winson, Harvey Kubernick, Andrei Codrescu, Lee Ballinger, Janet Hamill, Meri Danquah, Andy Clausen, Edwin Torres, Adriene Su, Ani DiFranco, Todd Colby, Dael Orlandersmith, Bern Porter, R. L. Burnside, Peter Lee, Junior Kimbrough, Dennis Downey, Eileen Myles, Patricia Smith, Michael Brown, Mary McCann, Edward Herrera, David Kodeski, Guillermo Gomez-Pena, Francisco Alarcon, Nathanial Mackey, Ishmael Reed, Kimiko Hahn, Sekou Sundiata, Julia Vinograd, Antler, Peter Pennekamp, Bruce Isaacson, Jen Joseph, Liz Balil, Mud Baron, Jayleen Sun, Chris Baswell, David Lehman, D. L. Melham, Douglas Crase, Haas Mroue, Lawrence Joseph, Joe Bruchac, Drum Hadley, Carrie Jamison, Merilene M. Murphy, Bowerbird Intelligentleperson, Jack Powers, Verta Mac Grosvenor, Jonathan Williams, James Baker Hall, George Tysh, Chris Tysh, Eugene Redmond, Ruby Lerner, Cyn Salach, Reno, Marvin Tate, Lewis MacAdams, Kurt Heintz, Seanna Watson. And a special thanks to Kim Witherspoon.

Acknowledgments

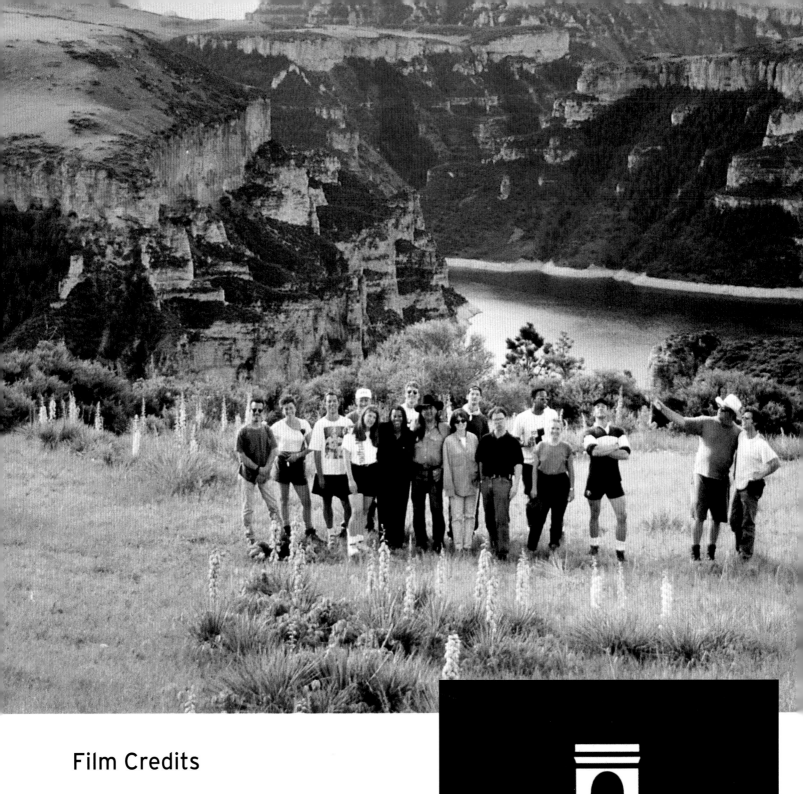

Film Credits

Directed by
MARK PELLINGTON

Produced and created by
JOSHUA BLUM
AND
BOB HOLMAN

Co-produced by
ANNE MULLEN

director of photography....**THOMAS KRUEGER**

editor....................**ADAM SCHWARTZ**

original music ....**TOMANDANDY**

production designer ....**STEVE KIMMEL**

design and typography...........**NUMBER 17**

on-line editor ....**FRED SALKIND**

project coordinator.........**COLETTE COYNE**

sound designer/mixer ....**MITCH OSIAS**

assistant editor/...............**TIM BARNES**
additional sound design

colorist....................**JOE SZUTARSKI**

Road crew

production manager . . . . HANNAH WITTICH

gaffer . . . . CORWIN BIBB

key grip . . . . ANTHONY ARNAUD

second camera . . . . {PETER AGLIATA
                                            {TAMI REIKER

a.c. . . . . {SUSANNA VIRTANEN
                                        {WILLIAM PERKINS

sound . . . . {TOM PAUL
                                  {JAN McLAUGHLIN

Road crew

key p.a . . . . SHERIE WELDON

p.a . . . . KEVIN F. ANDERSON

coach driver . . . . DARYL COCHRAN

project research . . . . RANI SINGH

office coordinator . . . . SHARON LYNCH

art director L.A. . . . . MAGGIE GOLDMAN

art director N.Y. . . . . JENNY ALEX

---

project development . . . . CAROLYN PEYSER

post production assistants . . . . . {LEE HARMON
                                      {MADELEINE BAILLIEU

editorial assistants . . . . {HEATHER LEVY
                                    {NATALIE MATANIC

assistant audio engineer . . . . JIM McNAMARA

Legal assistance

MARC CHAMLIN:
LOEB AND LOEB

ROSE H. SCHWARTZ, ERIC S. BROWN:
FRANKLIN, WEINRIB, RUDELL AND VASSALLO, P.C.

Key contributing vendors

filmed with ARRIFLEX cameras and lenses
supplied by CAMERA SERVICE CENTER

PRO-CAMERA LIGHTING AND RENTALS INC.

CHIMERA PHOTOGRAPHIC LIGHTING

KINO-FLO INC.

CECO INTERNATIONAL CORP.

fiscal sponsorship by MEDIA NETWORK

---

color lab
DUART FILM AND VIDEO LABORATORIES

black and white lab
BONO FILM AND VIDEO SERVICES INC.

off-line support
LOST PLANET EDITORIAL
ONESOURCE, INC.

negative matching
J.G. FILMS

post production services
IMAGE GROUP POST

support provided by
INDEPENDENT FEATURE PROJECT
EASTMAN KODAK COMPANY
CROSSROADS FILMS

FOR THE INDEPENDENT TELEVISION SERVICE

supervising producer
MARK LIPSON

production development
KATE LEHMANN

publicity
MICHAEL SHEPLEY PUBLIC RELATIONS

commissioning team
MARTHA CARRELL
PHIL LUCAS
SANDY MCLEOD
PETER H. PENNEKAMP
BARBARA L. TSUMAGARI